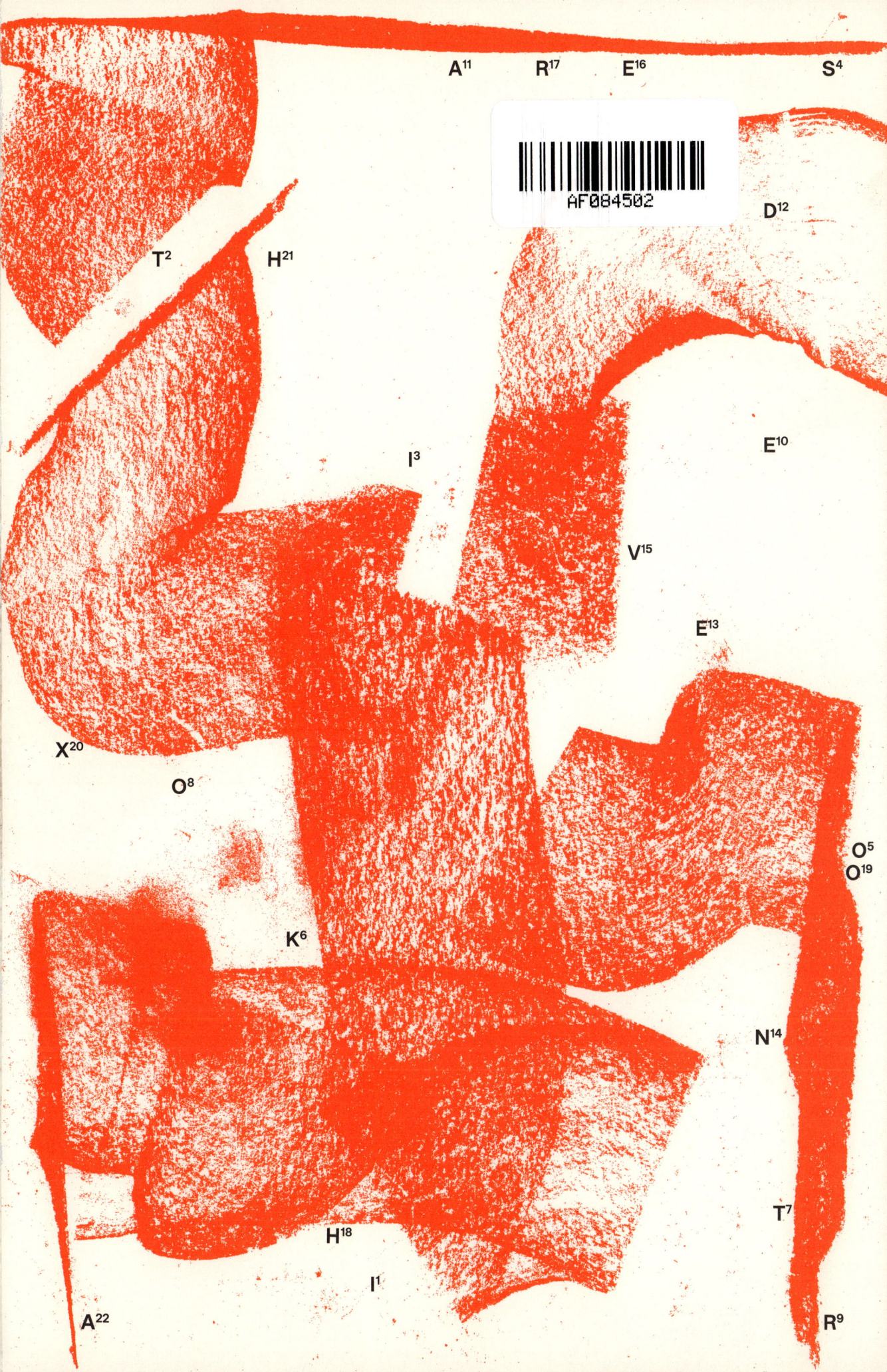

R[12] V[3] K[13]
OLU[4]

T[8]

HAHE[7]

R[1]

GJATË[9]

BRA[1]

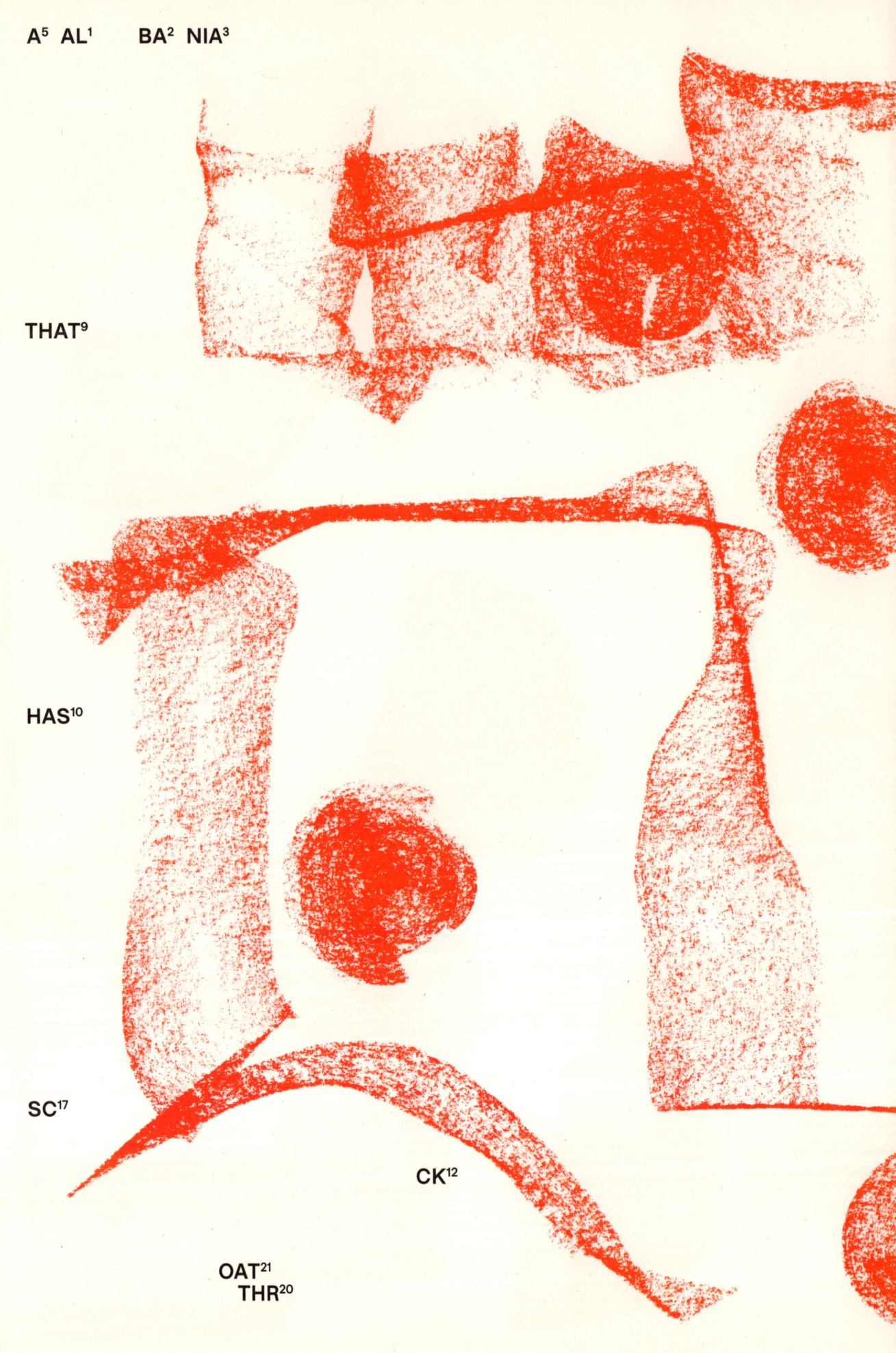

A[5] AL[1]   BA[2] NIA[3]

THAT[9]

HAS[10]

SC[17]

CK[12]

OAT[21]
THR[20]

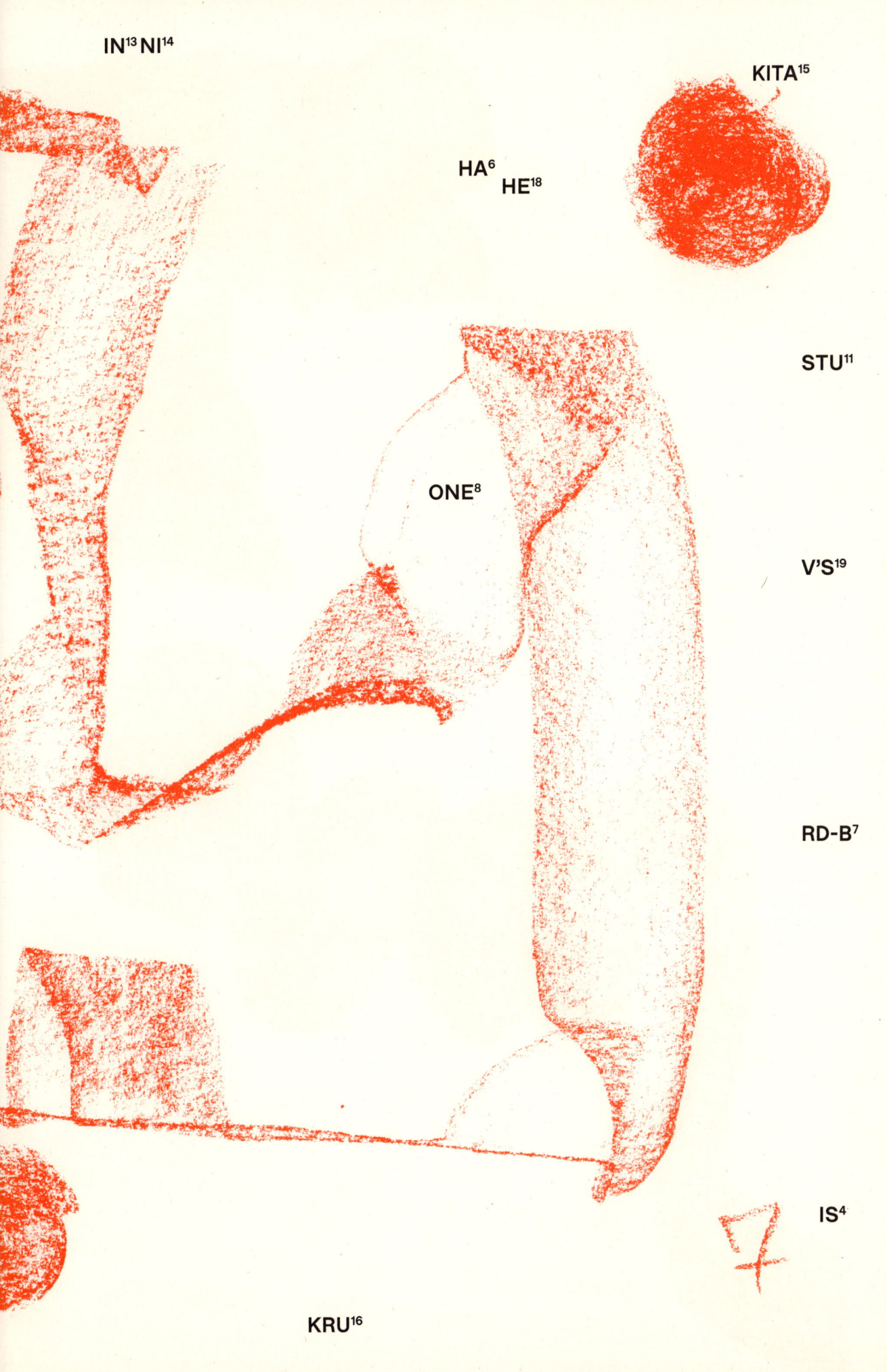

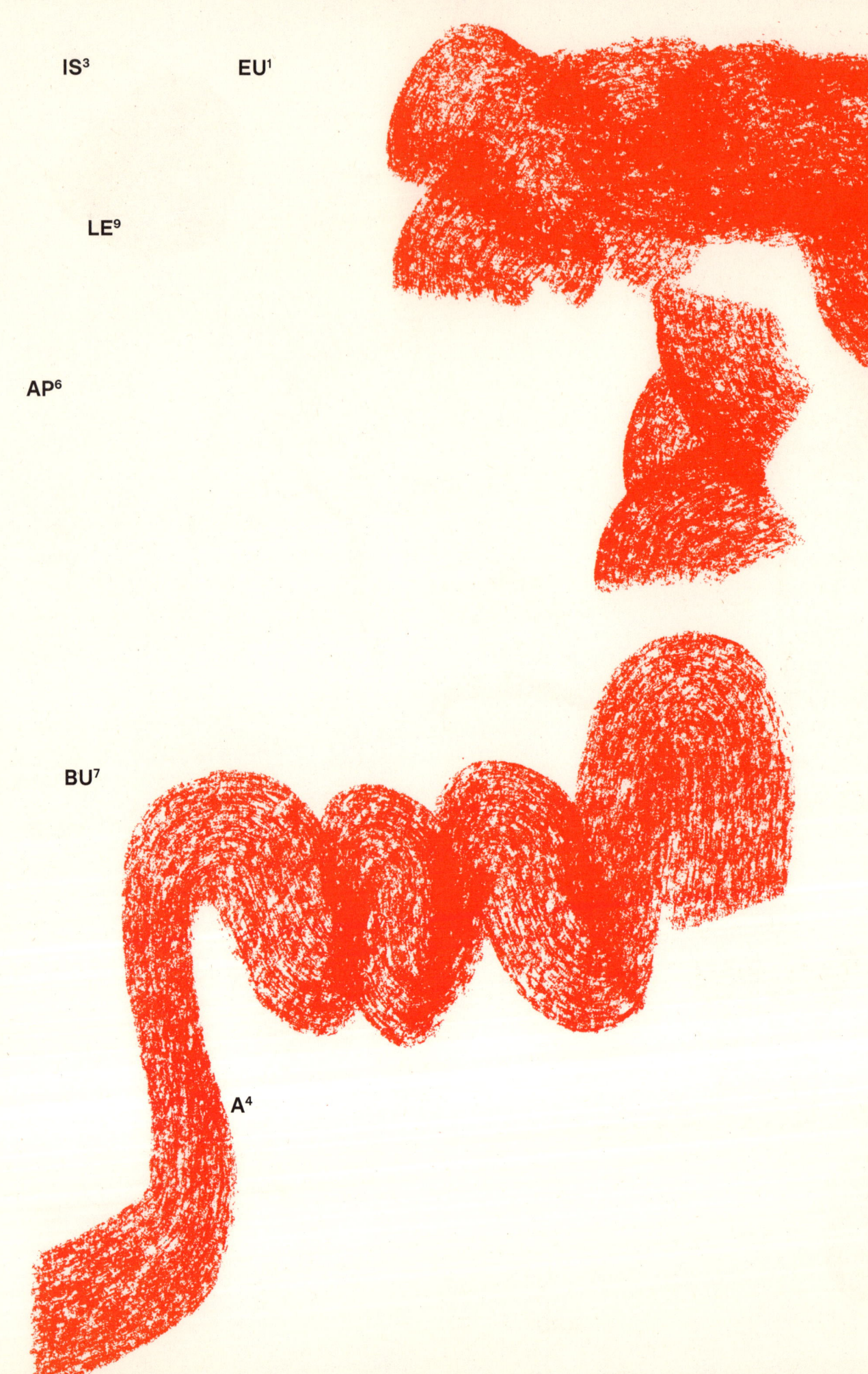

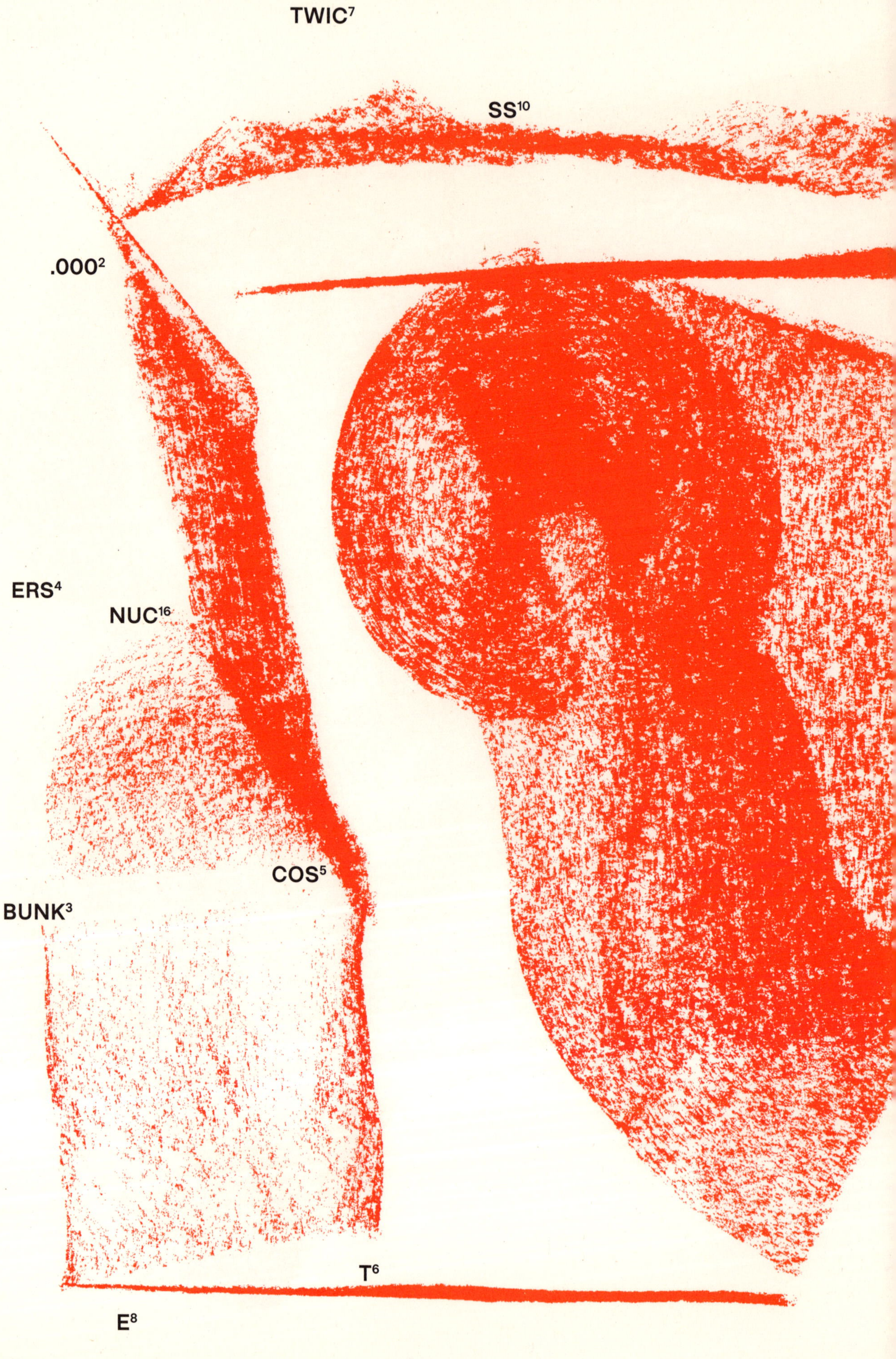

TWIC[7]

SS[10]

.000[2]

ERS[4]

NUC[16]

COS[5]

BUNK[3]

T[6]

E[8]

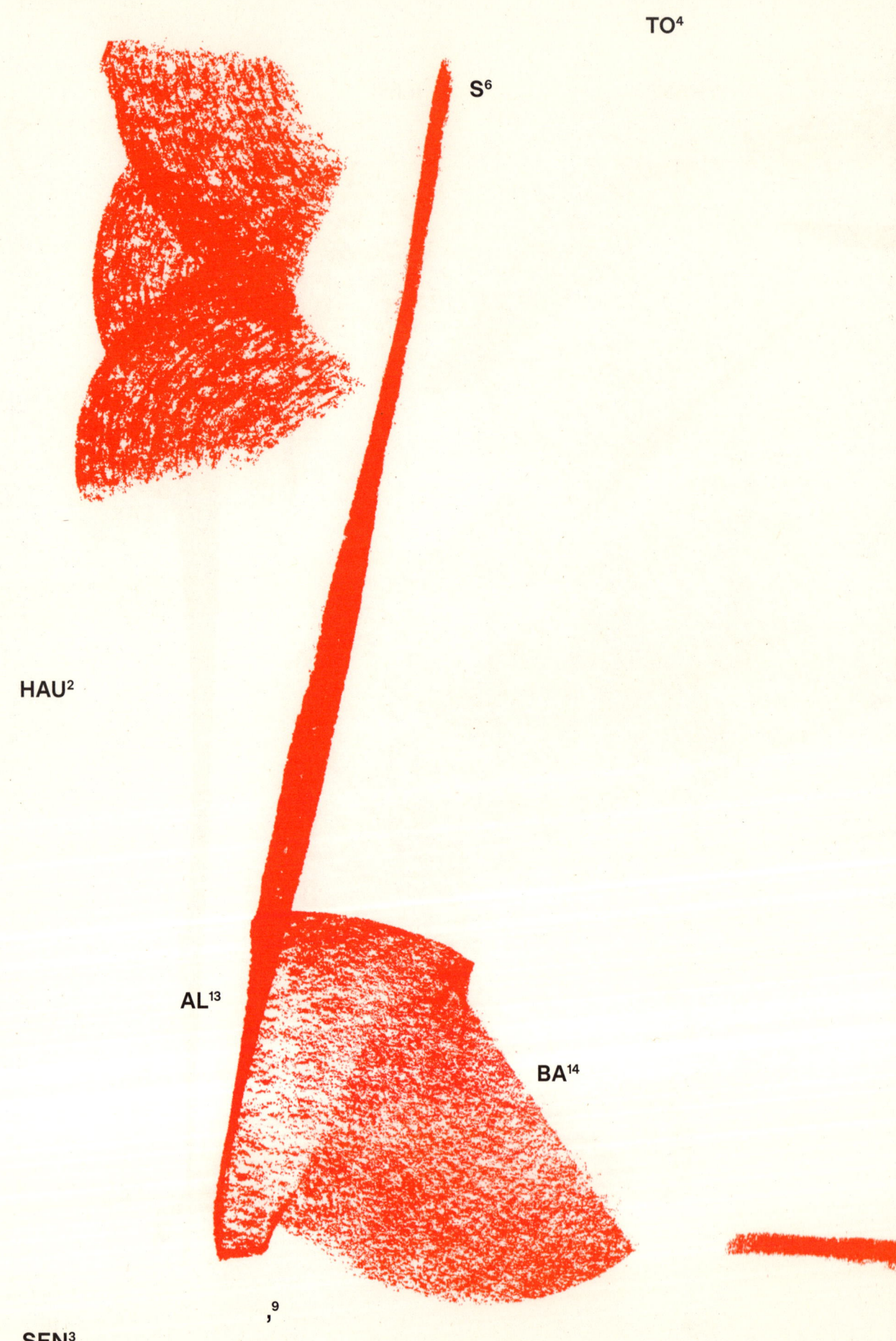

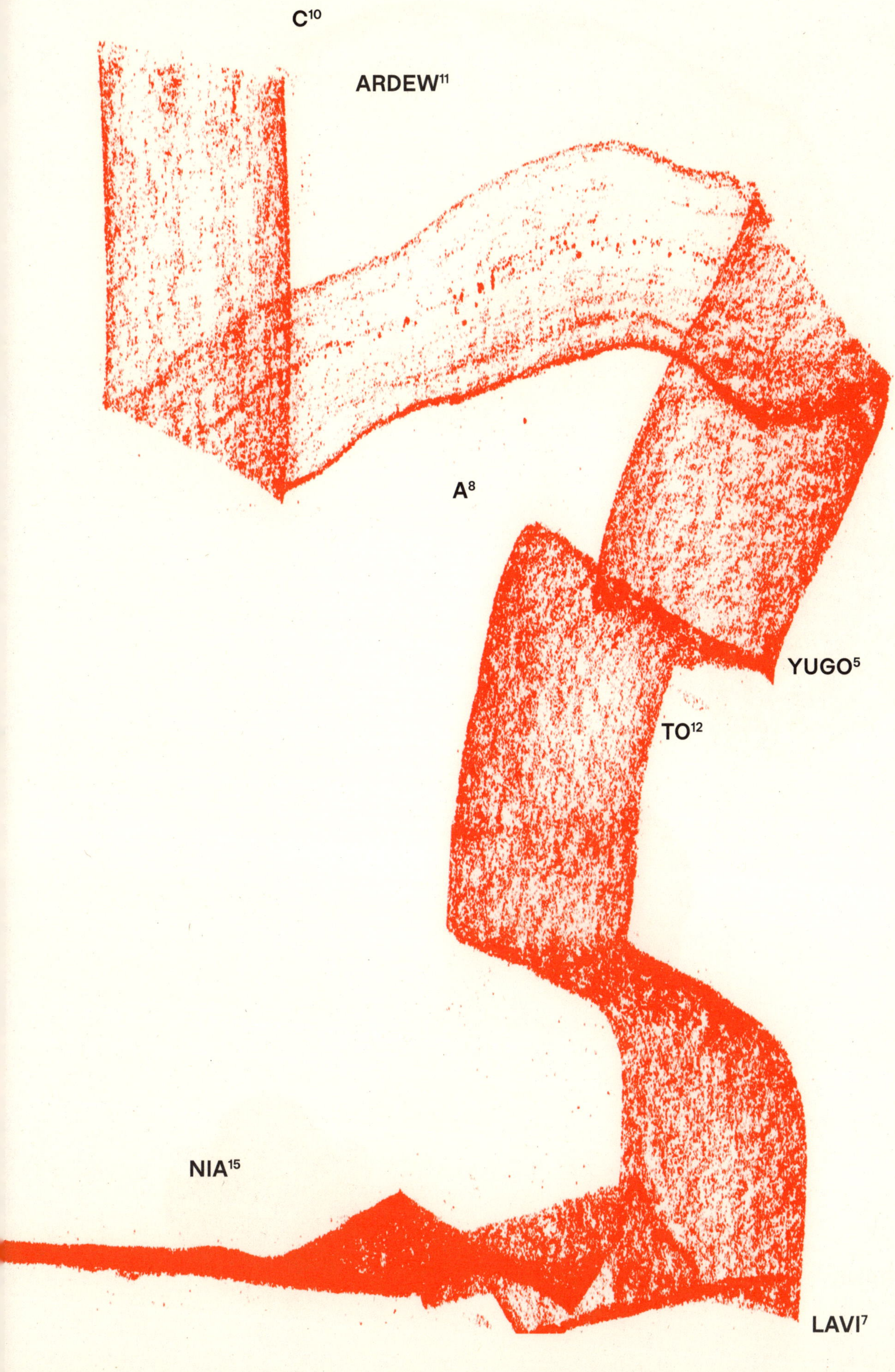

C[10]

ARDEW[11]

A[8]

YUGO[5]

TO[12]

NIA[15]

LAVI[7]

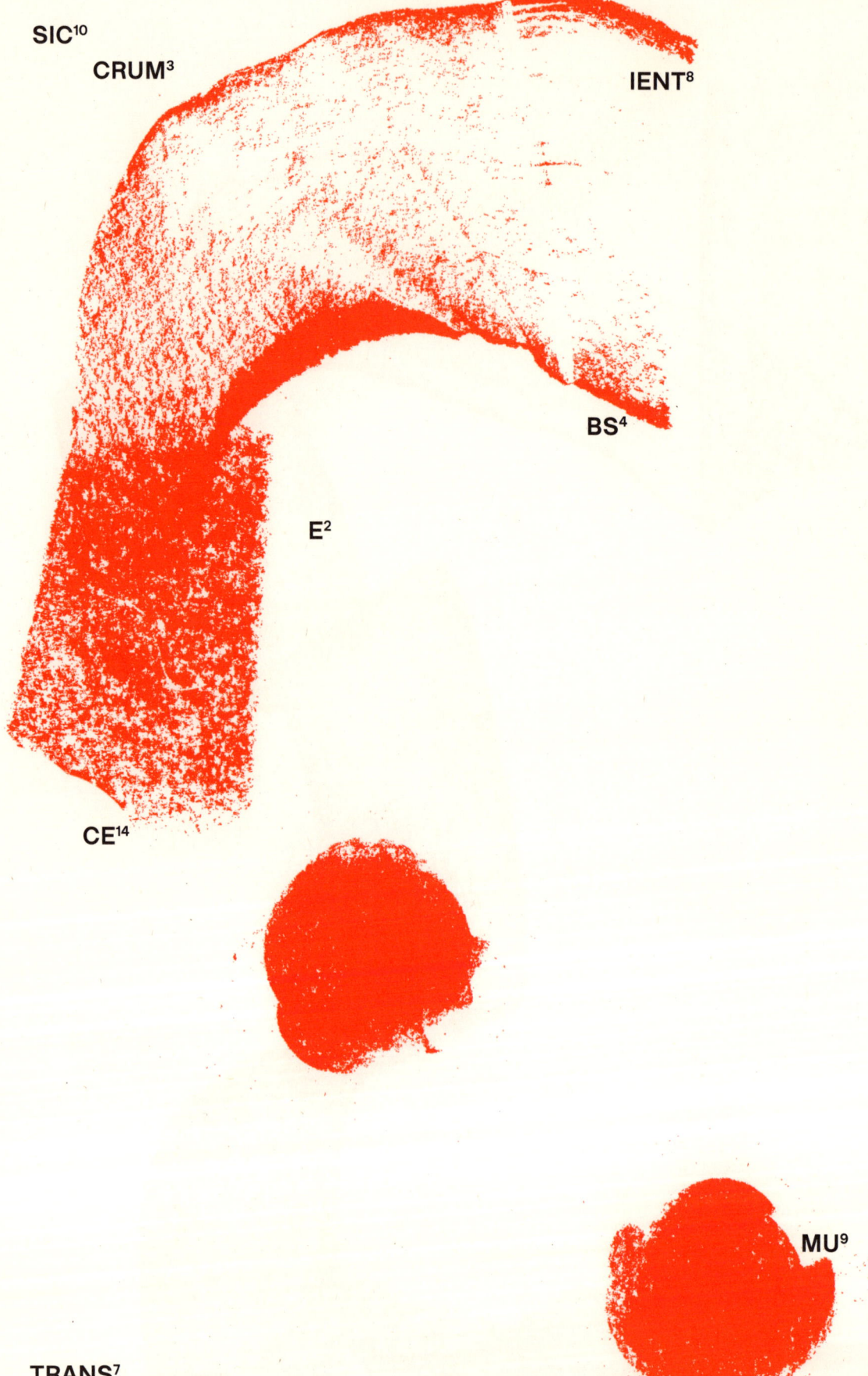

AL[11]

EX[12]

A[6]

ISTEN[13]

TH[1]

OF[5]

AL[11]

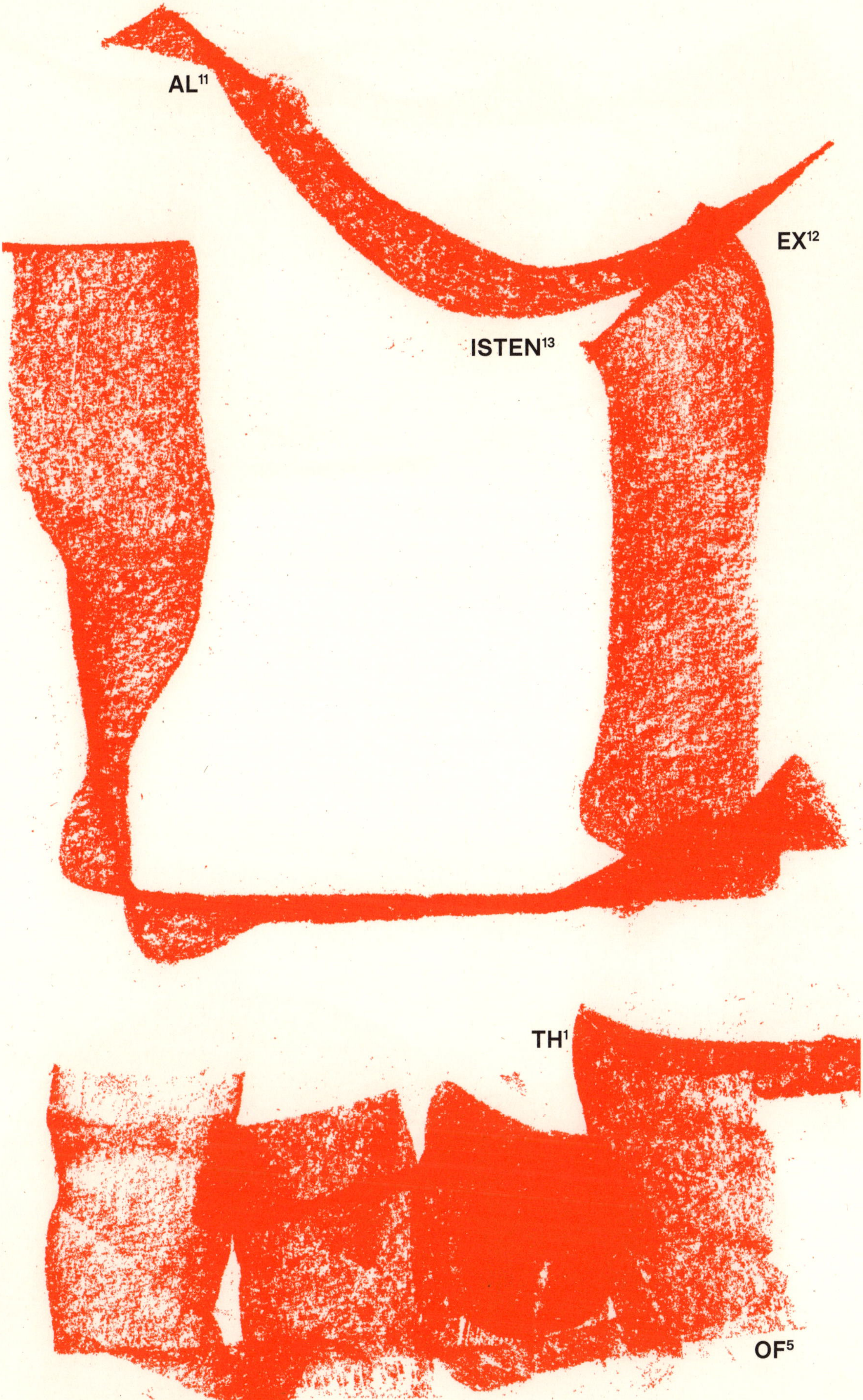

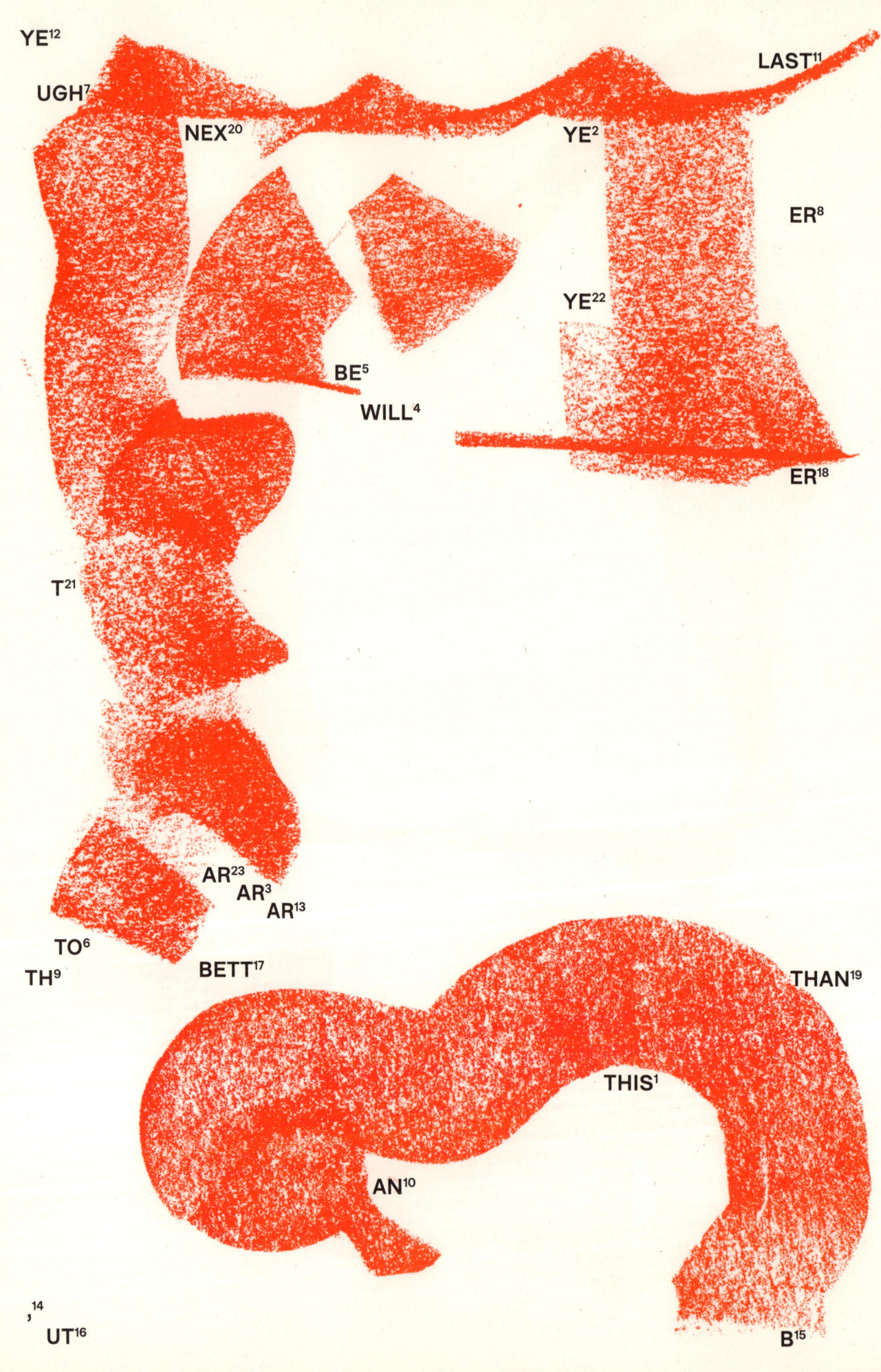

FROM SCRATCH
Albanian Summer Picaresque

CONTENT
1–16	Slogans (drawings by Ott Kagovere)
18–26	From Scratch to Scratch: The Story of *Albanian Summer*
27–38	Albania, 1973–1990: Interview with Dave Smith
39–62	Texts by Dave Smith
	Music in Albania
	Muzika në Shqipëri
	Institute of People's Culture
	Albanian Composers — Unique in Europe
	Kompozitorët Shqiptarë — Unikë Në Evropë
	Albanian Summer liner notes
63–65	The Music of Dave Smith
	(by Gavin Bryars, from *Albanian Summer* liner notes)
66–71	Picaresque Story: Interview with Jan Steele
72–80	Jan Steele and Janet Sherbourne *Albanian Summer* Scrapbook: reviews, concerts, promo materials, photos
81–112	Short Annotated Bibliography of International Publications on Albania
113–144	Photography Unmasks — Fotografia Demaskon (a selection from *Zëri i Rinisë*)

FROM SCRATCH TO SCRATCH
The Story of *Albanian Summer*

This is a story of *Albanian Summer: An Entertainment*, an album released by Practical Music in London in 1984. The album was composed by Dave Smith, performed by Janet Sherbourne and Jan Steele, and the liner notes were written by Gavin Bryars, who are among the most established musicians in the UK's experimental and improvised music scene. Smith, for example, was a member of The Scratch Orchestra, and collaborated with Cornelius Cardew on several occasions, while in 1976 Steele released a split album with John Cage, *Voices and Instruments,* on Brian Eno's label Obscure Records. In the seventies Bryars gained an international reputation with his compositions. The record *Albanian Summer* has one song on each side, and—as the promo material for Practical Music describes—is a combination of Albanian folk and classical music with a distinctly Kurt Weil style.

Jan Steele, in an interview published further in this volume, describes the music of *Albanian Summer* as "picaresque": a mode of storytelling with quickly-changing episodes where the hero moves from one adventure to another. This episodic style of narrative is exemplified by Don Quixote, in which the seemingly unconnected episodes are brought together by rough but appealing themes. The *Albanian Summer* album similarly takes form around traditional Albanian music, highlighting the ways it has appealed to British experimental musicians and progressive writers. Dave Smith, the album's composer, visited Albania regularly from 1973 to 1990, writing numerous essays on Albanian music and arranging Albanian songs for various musical projects. Simultaneously, Smith was involved in People's Liberation Music and Progressive Cultural Association: politically-engaged bands lead by Cardew who at that time was shifting socialist ideologies from Mao Zedong to Enver Hoxha. Smith was also in communication with A.L. "Bert" Lloyd, a musician and folklorist who had been a member of the Communist Party of Great Britain as early as the thirties, and who in 1966 compiled an album called *Folk Music in Albania*. The album was released by Topic Records, the oldest independent record label in the world founded in 1939 by the Workers' Music Association. At the same time, Dave Smith was a member of the Albanian Society and contributed to its journal *Albanian Life*, which was run and edited by Bill Bland. Bland was a member of various Marxist-Leninist organisations in Britain and has written numerous essays on Albania, co-authored a book on Anglo-American relations with Albania, and compiled the first annotated bibliography on Albania in English.

Albanian Summer is therefore the product of a deeply complex artistic and political network. It is difficult to conceive of a neat and clean narrative with so many layers of histories involved. Complicating the situation even further is that the ethics to which these artistic and theoretical practices ascribed to have little value in our times. Today, both the United Kingdom and Albania are members of the North Atlantic Treaty Organisation (NATO) and Organisation for Security and Co-operation in Europe (OSCE), but from 1939 to 1991, the two countries did not have any diplomatic relations.

Albania was the only country in Europe, and among the few in the entire world (others being North Korea and Guatemala) which the UK did not have any diplomatic relations with. There were numerous reasons for the cut between two countries, some related to Albania itself, others to the imperialist legacy of Britain and the competing tensions in the Cold War superpowers' networks.

Cornelius Cardew, a major influence to Smith's musical maturation, never visited Albania. However, the Revolutionary Communist Party of Britain Marxist-Leninist (RCPB ML) to which he belonged from 1974 onwards (and was also a member of its Central Committee from 1978) had sided with the Party of the Labour of Albania (PLA) during their split with the People's Republic of China. In other words, the Marxist-Leninism of Cardew's party, based in London, aligned with Albania in political matters regarding how contemporary Marxist-Leninism interpreted the international developments. In an email conversation, Dave Smith remembered in 1980 mentioning to Cardew that he was contemplating or composing something "with an Albanian flavour" (this would be *Albanian Summer* in fact). Cardew immediately criticised the idea. This might be the reason that Albania, for Cardew, was not a cultural but political influence. Nevertheless, Cardew's trajectory traversing art and politics was important not only to Smith, but to all musicians, regardless their political stance.

Cardew pushed the boundaries of musical abstraction into unforeseen dimensions by completely abandoning notations in favour of his own original graphic scores. His works such as *Treatise* and *The Great Learning*, as well as his involvement in The Scratch Orchestra, introduced new ways of engagement with experimental music, which were democratic, participatory, and outside of traditional musical institutions. Cardew's work embraced a true spirit of experimentation, and as Dave Smith and many others have commented, the open aspect of his work was bound to end in Leftists politics. Perhaps what is difficult to grasp from today's perspective is how this political engagement ended in the Enverist spectrum of the Left. One could imagine that the author of the 'Draft Constitution of the Scratch Orchestra [1969]', calling for "enthusiasts pooling of resources and assembling for action (music making, performance, edification)," would ascribe his social engagement to some kind of open-ended—if not anarchist—version of Trotskyist leftism.

Cardew's involvement with the Marxist-Leninism of Enver Hoxha cannot be explained with art alone, or with the formal and ethical aspect of his previous musical work. Cardew's politicisation also signalled compositionally a moving away from an emphasis on form towards content. The conversion towards content was so strong that it manifested itself in rewriting the previous avant-garde principles [i.e. revising *The Great Learning* with Maoist slogans, publishing a book against his own mentors *Stockhausen Serves Imperialism*, etc.] Particularly revealing of this trend is a lecture by Cardew after the performance of his earlier avant-garde piece *The Great Learning* during his Enverist period in an art gallery in 1977. Cardew opposed the bourgeois ideology which he believed was giving primacy to form over content by pointing to the abstract paintings exhibited on the walls of the gallery, which he interpreted as meaningless. He insisted that political art, on the other hand, necessitated clear language, understanding, and accessibility. He stated:

> When I play political music [in that particular case *Thälmann Variations*, from 1974], I am saying to you what actually is the case. This music is about Ernst Thälmann. It uses the materials that developed culturally around Thälmann, around the issue of Thälmann, and how he fought against the fascists before the Second World War, and nobody is going to tell me any different.[1]

What, then, would be these "materials that developed culturally" and socially around Cardew in the seventies? They were the imperialist legacy of the UK, the national-chauvinism of the British monarchy, the "physical and mental devastation which capitalism inflicted upon working people," the absence of political revolution, and the alienation of working people from political music. These were just a handful of reasons why individuals like Cardew expressed a global sense of crisis that transcended national development: to them, there became no need to visit Third World countries to experience the misery of the exploited people when socio-economic exploitation seemed to pervade every nation.[2] One might agree with Coriún Aharonián, an Uruguayan experimental musician, who retrospectively wrote that "what becomes evident is that imperial England was, during the 1970s, as provincial as Nicaragua or Albania. Only this fact can explain Cardew's lack of a stronger discussion about what he was doing. The difference is that imperial culture acquired through his scholarly training allowed him to really believe he was doing something important for his historical moment."[3] In other words, Cardew thought always in extremes, and his pioneering experiments, artistic and political, influenced many around him.

Dave Smith joined The Scratch Orchestra in 1971 at a pivotal moment of debate, about whether the collective's programming and activities were matching each other. The discontent and discord that these meetings sowed ultimately helped to generate a more radical politicising of experimental music. Some members of The Scratch Orchestra, Smith included, continued with the People's Liberation Music (PLM) and the more overtly political Progressive Cultural Association (PCA). These groups advocated the importance of content even further. The point was to introduce lines of demarcation against the endless revisionism of sophisticated apolitical abstract art, and be as precise as possible towards the heart of matters through art. As one might anticipate, the anti-revisionist ideology brewing in Albania became an important reference in this new shift. Cardew's note from 1975 stating that "Artistic thinking these days is an endless process of finessing without interest," could be easily juxtaposed with Enver Hoxha's commentary from the same period stating that "Every day 'new' major or minor schools of thought appear like innumerable religious sects and heresies. Nevertheless, they have a common philosophical basic—idealism—with all its endless refinements." John Tilbury, British experimental musician and biographer of Cardew who further supported this comparison, added in commentary: "The fact that as the art becomes more mindlessly 'refined' the sponsors become more consciously right-wing."[4]

The connection between Albanian politics and some members of The Scratch Orchestra had become equally theoretical as it was historical. Dave Smith, who participated in concerts of PLM and to some extent PCA, has provided musical entries describing this widely shared interest in Albania. In his 1975 tour of the United States and Canada, alongside *Thälmann Variations*, Cardew also performed transcriptions of Albanian songs arranged by Smith, including "Eagle of the Guerillas." A 1976 concert of PCA also included five anti-fascist songs arranged for piano solo by Smith, also incorporating Albanian themes. During that same year, Cardew wrote a piece called "Vietnam Sonata," incorporating three themes: "The Song of the National Liberation Front of South Vietnam" (symbolising self-reliance), the Albanian song "The Heroic Vietnam" (referencing the fraternal support of the socialist countries of Vietnam and Albania) and "The People of Vietnam," a song written by members of the Kreuzberg Vietnam Committee in West Berlin (signifying the internationalism and solidarity of the democratic people in the imperialist heartlands). "The Heroic Vietnam", largely inspired by Albanian folk music, was arranged by Smith.

During this period of composing anti-fascist songs and arrangements inspired by Albanian music, Smith was also a close collaborator in serial, processual, and minimal experimental music works together with John White, Michael Parsons, and Christopher Hobbs. He was a member of the Garden Furniture Music Ensemble, involved in the projects of Gavin Bryars, and composed "wall-of-sound" minimalist works like *Diabolus Maximus* for five pianos in 1976.[5] In his overview of the history of British experimental music after Cardew, Richard Barrett, discusses Smith's work as an example of "committed music," combining the "popular" and "folk" in new ways, as in *Albanian Summer*, which was not driven by the prevailing postmodernism of the eighties but was a sincere engagement. As Barrett states, "The use of well-worn stylistic characteristics is a matter of his own *innate preference* rather than a striking of a populist pose."[6] Topics around Albania were certainly Dave Smith's innate preference. He was a frequent contributor to the *Albanian Life: Journal of the Albanian Society*, and in 1986 he was elected committee-member of the Albanian Society in Britain. The Society's president at the time was musicologist A.L. Lloyd, while its secretary was a militant activist Bill Bland. The work of these two figures provided much of the context to Smith's future work.

William "Bill" Bland was a persistent Marxist-Leninist figure active in communist organisations in New Zealand and the UK from the fifties onwards. He was one of the first to criticise the British Road to Socialism, already in 1951, and when Albania openly broke with China in 1978, unlike most Marxist-Leninist thinkers at the time, he took the side of Albania and through Albanian Society established the official contacts with the Party of Labour of Albania. He wrote:

> At that time [1978] the one person who still had contacts with the Albanians was the expert on folk music, the president of our society Bert Lloyd. Bert Loyd made regular trips to Albania to record folk music, not as president of the Albania Society but in a personal capacity. We asked him if he would point out to the Albanians on his next visit that it was rather ridiculous to have no Albania friendship society because there was no one except for ourselves, with whom they would not speak.[7]

This is how Bland and the Albanian Society established a political relationship with Albania, which was the only organisation in the UK having such connection. One of the primary agendas of the Society was to establish diplomatic relationships between two countries. The Albanian Society pursued an independent line in this, refusing to replicate what the majority of British media and expert literature had to say about Albania. Through the pages of *Albanian Life*, the Society members tirelessly opposed the official, globally-dominant views of Albania—challenging the often repeated mantras about lack of human rights, lack of democracy, and hysteria on the ban of religion. They wrote about folk music, theatre, and cultural institutions with interpretations seldom heard in the public sphere. This engagement also included translation of poetry, stories, texts on art, and reproduction of paintings produced in Albania. Not always were the Society's views on the official Party of the Labour shared: *Albanian Life* journal helped develop the practice of writing that was not only giving a new perspective on the socialist Albania, but also demolished many historical myths involving Britain's past. One of them was a book that the Albanian Society published together with The Albanian Friendship Society of Southern Californiain 1986 as *A Tangled Web: A History of Anglo-American Relations with Albania, 1912-1955*, written by William Bland and Ian Price. The book aims to demonstrate, through an abundance of archival materials, that the "conduct of Britain and the United States towards Albania—both before and after the establishment of the socialist regime—has been one of the most sordid and discreditable in the history of these Powers." *A Tangled Web* is "a story of the enforced partition of Albania; of the imposition of foreign rulers on the Albanian state; of the perversion of truth and justice (in the case of the Corfu Incident) in an effort to make Albania the scapegoat for the crimes of others; of the embezzlement of Albania's gold reserve by Britain; of concerted attempts to ostracise Albania from international organisations."[8] The evidence and the narrative of the book has impressed respected historians of Albania like Peter R. Prifti, and still today is read as a serious work on the persistence of modern colonialism in the Balkans.

Bland was an attentive reader of Enver Hoxha, and as such, *A Tangled Web* was written to prove through archival research Hoxha's statement in *The Anglo-American Threat to Albania,* that "the imperialists and world reaction have never ceased for one day or even one minute [to work] against our country" was "in no way [an] exaggeration."[9] Apart from Bland and Price, Hoxha's other devoted readers included Cornelius Cardew who, in Hoxha, found a strong argument for the belief in the actuality of communism. In one of his last speeches at the meeting of RCPB ML in London, Cardew insisted on using art and music to create a new world of socialism, which he described as "an immediate aim" against "savage, aggressive and exploitative policies of imperialists." As a conclusion to the speech, Cardew quoted Hoxha by saying: "The world is at a state when the cause of revolution and national liberation of peoples is not just an aspiration and future prospect, but a problem taken up for solution."[10]

The world of socialism had entered the eighties compromising with the bourgeois norms, capitalist institutions, and obscurantist postmodernist theories. Isolated from the objectives of the world, Hoxha had detected these deviations and fiercely denounced new socialist projects as revisionist restorators of capitalism and imperialism. Hoxha was, as Jan Halliday writes in his book *The Artful Albanian*, "extremely observant" of the actions of "revisionist" leaders of USSR, China, Yugoslavia, Romania, and exposing the secret diplomacy of British and American imperialists.[11] He was especially critical towards the rising armament industry and the militarisation of world politics. In this regard, he did not distinguish between the West and the East, between capitalists and socialist blocs, NATO and Warsaw Treaty, and bourgeois-imperialists and social-imperialists. Hoxha's consistently firm and resolutely anti-militarist stance, and unconditional support for world peace, is deserving of further attention and study. Hoxha's popularity and the resonance of his texts in the eighties was through his strong anti-nuclear position, which, especially in the first half of the eighties, was echoing the mass mobilisation against the serious threat of the nuclear arsenal to the whole human civilisation. In the background of two superpowers—the NATO and Warsaw Treaty—and the deployment of Pershing II and SS-20 missiles in Europe, the youth in the West emerged as a political force. Enver Hoxha's commentary on this in his "political diary" strangely resembles statements of E.P. Thompson and END (European Nuclear Disarmament) from that same period:

> The powerful demonstration against 'Euro-missiles' which have been going on in Western Europe for some days now, as well as the silent opposition of the peoples of Eastern Europe, are very good signs of the mounting awareness among peoples of the very great danger with which the two imperialist superpowers, the United States of America and the Soviet Union, are threatening them.[12]

Halliday commenting on Hoxha's "brutal frankness" says: "He really does spill the beans." Compared to other socialist leaders, he is an avid reader and "he thinks."[13] The question is what can one learn from his writings, which the avant-garde art theoretician Peter Wollen noted contain "the rich vein of gold"?[14] Can we today find anything relevant in all these experiments, delusions, and extremely vigilant observations? What can one learn from the communist leader who operated in the fundamental Manichean world where Marxism-Leninism is always good, revisionism bad; in other words, where Stalin is always right, and all the rest wrong? This black-and-white capitulation is Hoxha's theoretical cul de sac. Also, as Halliday rightly observed, in these issues "Hoxha is entirely predictable and often boring,"[15] and, could be added, often wrong. In other words, how does one read and engage with Hoxha beyond his "Stalinist hallucinations?" Or, as Arshi Pipa wrote, how can one read his work without getting dizzy from Hoxha's mixed-up theories and explanations.[16] Pipa calls this "Hoxha's theory of causative attraction," referring to arbitrary and ad hoc explanations that are going on in his mind—understandable only to a few dedicated communists. At the bottom of this world view is the perception of liberalism as a disease which can be prevented with vigilance: a distillation of the form of Hoxha's theoretical discourse. His theories imagine communism as a pure and crystallised ideology, discovering revisionism in every step, including in the world of the communist party apparatus. As many commentators have observed, Hoxha did not lack a sense of self-criticism, and he was genuinely against empty phrases and "balloony" slogans. Problems stemmed from the issue that this vigilance and discipline was felt heavier at home, especially by not-so-communist citizens. As Arshi Pipa writes, "The forty years of uninterrupted Stalinism have left scars in almost every aspect of Albanian life and culture. Albanian art is crudely primitive (with the occasional exception of music); Albanian literature has remained with the prison-house of socialist realism; economics has been reduced to a 'science' of increasing percentages," and so on, with multiple other accusations. "This is not to argue that Hoxha's record has been completely negative," adds Pipa, observing that "there have been achievements in agriculture and industry; diseases are under control; the social status of women has greatly improved; illiteracy has nearly disappeared." To this he also adds that the policies of bridging the gaps between city and countryside had been considerably advanced: "The means of production are owned and supervised by a state that is entirely controlled by the Labour Party. The aristocratic and bourgeois families of the times of King Zog and the fascist-Nazi occupation have long been liquidated..."[17] The question is whether it was "necessary to pay such a high price" for such accelerated and secular modernisation.[18] Or if we formulate in another way: whether it was necessary for the prison-house of feudal Albania to be demolished at the expense of bourgeois and dissident artists and intellectuals? Dave Smith's answer is that this new system that emerged from scratch had its own culture, in some areas, especially in music, emerging with much more open and egalitarian institutions than its Western counterparts. Enver Hoxha's socialist Albania was certainly a prison-house for bourgeois culture and its remnants in an ancient regime mentality. Albanian communism was unprecedented in this regard. Looking at world affairs from this perspective introduces a new predicate to the language against the narrative of super-imperialist hegemony.

After the fall of socialism, Jan Faber Mient, who was the General Secretary of the Inter-Church Peace Council (a mass non-aligned peace platform in Holland) wrote that the ex-socialist countries in the post-nineties would need to "start from scratch."[19] Liberated from "Leninist political systems," these new regimes faced the need to adapt to the pluralism of a "market economy." Faber, who was also a co-Chairman of the Helsinki Citizens Assembly for Peace and Democracy, did consider the possibilities of detente (peaceful co-existence) and European cooperation in the conditions of the post-nineties. Faber, and many activists in the ranks of European Nuclear

Disarmament and dissident socialists, were eager to find the ways to re-activate the Helsinki Accords of 1975 in the new circumstances. Some previous socialist countries like Czechoslovakia and GDR showed interest in this idea, nurturing the belief to apply the Accords to a new political landscape under the guise of the newly established Helsinki Citizens Assembly. But where was Albania in these conversations? As it is known, the term 'Helsinki' here refers to the 1975 Helsinki Accords, better known as the Conference on Security and Co-operation, the high point of detente in the seventies where was first "made link between security and human rights." All European countries, except for Albania signed the Helsinki Accords, which turned out to be one of the most important agreements for the future of Europe. *Zëri i Popullit* dubbed the Helsinki conference as "the conference of insecurity in Europe," and Enver Hoxha wrote that Albania didn't get the stain of "Helsinki mud," describing the Helsinki Accords as "a document of more than 200 pages that says nothing."[20] After 1991, this abstinence from the European future turned out to be a heavy debt to pay for entering the West.

In 1962, after its split from the Soviet Union and allegiance with China, Arshi Pipa wrote in an emigree magazine in the US that for Albania "the locus cannot but be in the Western world, in the part of it inhabited by European families of nations."[21] Thirty years after this, when James Baker, the Secretary of the United States, visited Tirana told a massive crowd gathered to greet him: "You have made the first great breakthroughs to begin rejoining the community of nations after long decades of cruel, self-imposed isolation." Baker added the price for joining this "community of nations": The privatisation of agriculture and industry, the decisive opening of the country to foreign investment, long-overdue policies to allow a convertible currency, liberalised prices, and a balanced national budget that would be essential in laying the groundwork for Albania's eventual economic recovery.[22]

No matter how theoretically hard-lined it might sound, the commentary of Alain Badiou in *The Communist Hypothesis* that we should not "give any ground in the contexts of criminalization and hair-raising anecdotes in which the forces of reaction always tried to invalidate communists," including Marx, Lenin, Mao Zedong, Tito, and Enver Hoxha, is actual than ever.[23] In our world of aggressive capitalism spreading to every corner of society, ravaging the entire earth, drying up any possible human and animal existence, and systematically annihilating anything common, the observation of Enver Hoxha on December 31st in 1984 that "life confirms that capitalists are like baskets of crabs which tear at one another without mercy or ceremony," deserves contemporary attention. Hoxha's vision of communism and the practice of socialism in Albania will continue to be the source of "hair-raising anecdotes" against the Left. Here, in this volume, we present the narrative that might, to some extent, distort this view. What follows is a story of the Western world, seen from the perspective of Albania through the lenses of experimental musicians.

NOTES

1. John Tilbury, *Cornelius Cardew: A Life Unfinished*, Essex: Copula, 2008, p. 850.
2. Tilbury, *Cornelius Cardew*, p. 706.
3. Coriún Aharonián, 'Cardew as a Basis for a Discussion on Ethical Options', *Leonardo Music Journal, Vol. 11*, 2001, p. 15.
4. Tilbury, *Cornelius Cardew*, p. 665, 726.
5. For further information about Smith's musical works one can check the Experimental Music Catalogue site run by Virginia Anderson, and her PhD thesis *Aspects of British Experimental Music as a Separate Art-Music Culture*, London: University of London, 2004.
6. Richard Barrett, 'Avant-Garde and Ideology in the United Kingdom since Cardew', *New Music, Aesthetics and Ideology*, edited by Mark Delaere, Wilhelmshaven: Florian Noetzel, 1995, p. 267.
7. Interview with William B. Bland (1994), published for the first time in the Encyclopaedia of Anti-Revisionism On-Line. Transcribed, edited, and proofread by Sam Richards and Paul Saba. https://www.marxists.org/history/erol/uk.firstwave/bland-interview.htm
8. William Bland and Ian Price, *A Tangled Web: A History of Anglo-American Relations with Albania, 1912-1955*, London: Albanian Society and The Albanian Friendship Society of Southern California, 1986, p. i.
9. Bland and Price, *A Tangled Web*, p. 298.
10. Cornelius Cardew, 'Speech of Party Representative at International Youth Concert, London, 9th august 1980', *Cornelius Cardew: A Reader*, edited by Edwin Prévost, Essex: Copula, 2006, p. 274.
11. Jan Halliday, *The Artful Albanian: Memoirs of Enver Hoxha*, London: Chatto & Windus, 1986, p. 12.
12. Enver Hoxha, *The Superpowers, 1959-1984: Extracts from the Political Diary*, Tirana: 8 Nëntori, 1986, p. 643.
13. Halliday, *The Artful Albanian*, p. 8.
14. Halliday, *The Artful Albanian*, p. i.
15. Halliday, *The Artful Albanian*, p. 7.
16. Arshi Pipa, *Albanian Stalinism: Ideo-Political Aspects*, Boulder: East European Monographs, 1990, p. 112.
17. Arshi Pipa, 'The Political Culture of Hoxha's Albania', *The Stalinist Legacy*, edited by Tariq Ali, London: The Pelican Books, 1984, p.454.
18. Pipa, *Albanian Stalinism*, p. 122.
19. Jan Faber Mient, "Good Morning Europe!", *Europe from Below: An East-West Dialogue*, edited by Mary Kaldor, London: Verso, 1991, p. 140.
20. Hoxha, *The Superpowers*, p. 418-419.
21. Pipa, *Albanian Stalinism,* p. 40.
22. "25th Anniversary of Secretary of State James A. Baker's Historic Visit in Albania", https://medium.com/u-s-embassy-tirana/25th-anniversary-of-secretary-of-state-james-a-baker-iiis-historic-visit-in-albania-c2d363b9954e
23. Alain Badiou, *The Communist Hypothesis*, translated by David Macey and Steve Corcoran, London: Verso, 2010, p. 264.

ALBANIA, 1973-1990
Interview with Dave Smith

[Dave Smith talks, off-record, about his recent engagements in teaching with school children, teaching and preparing shows with Gamelan and steel pans.]

Q   Could you please tell us how you got interested in Albania? For instance, tell us more about your first visit there?

DAVE   Already at school I was aware that Albania was a rather strange place, because it is this small country in Europe, which is pro-Chinese. I am talking about 1963-64 here. The general idea was that it is a country that we knew nothing about, we didn't even know at that time that Britain had no diplomatic relations with Albania. It's the size of Wales, on good terms with China, a weird place, people's knowledge on Albania ended there. They were very much into independence. This was my view on Albania, very general, like anyone else. In the early seventies, further interest came from political reasons. Political awakening of that time, all sorts of leftist, quite a few Marxist-Leninist groups, were influential. In 1973, I lived near a place called Bellman Books, which was near Tufnell Park in London. That was the headquarters of the Communist Party of Britain Marxist-Leninist, which still exists. The leading light was a bloke called Reg Birch, whom I never met. He was a leading trade unionist in engineering, but there were a couple of other characters whom I got to know slightly, there was a guy called Bill (William) Ash, who died not so long ago. He had quite a war record, he was I think an Airforce pilot.

Q   Is he the one who wrote a book on Albania?

DAVE   Yes, *Pickaxe and Rifle: The Story of Albanian People*.

Q   I remember it being very affirmative towards Enver Hoxha.

DAVE   Oh, yes. It is a book written very much from that side. Certainly more than any other book written in English. He was an interesting character. He wrote an autobiography called *Red Square*. I think he worked at BBC; he might be discriminated against because of his political views. Anyway, the woman who worked there, Dorothy Birch, was married to Reg Birch, and she was running the bookshop. She told me once when I was there that the Regent Holidays were arranging trips to Albania. So, I followed it up, and went to Albania. This was in 1973. I spent a week in the tourist complex in Durrës, and also spent a week in Saranda. I didn't get to Korçë on that trip. I think I went to the usual places, Kruja, Shkodra, Tirana. So, yes, that was the introduction. On that trip I met . . . Ian Price, who now lives in Los Angeles. He sort of led me to folk music . . . broadcast on Radio Tirana, particularly one programme at 5 am, which was the length of a side of a cassette, which was 45 minutes. On future trips what I did was to set the alarm to 5 o'clock in the morning, set the cassette recording and go back to sleep. So, my folk music knowledge is thanks to recording stuff from Radio Tirana. Occasionally one could hear some music live, for example there would be a concert of a group in the hotel in Saranda (in 1973), or we were taken to a big concert in Durrës (in 1987).

    I went several times to Albania between 1973 to 1990. It was '73, '77, '79, '80, '81, '82, '83, '84, '87, '88, and '90. These were arranged trips (with regent

Holidays or Skanderbeg Reisen): once I went with Steve Day (in 1990) on our own, with an individual visa, as a two man Albanian Society delegation.

Q   Who was arranging these trips?

DAVE   The Albanian Society, which doesn't exist anymore. I am not sure when they did stop. They just stopped sending their journal *Albanian Life*. It seems there is no record on the internet at all. I know one person involved in it, Neil Taylor. He worked for Regent Holidays, and he was also a member of Albanian Society, and he is also a member of old Albanian Friendship Society in England, which was, if not Zogist, certainly not pro-Enver. They still exist. Neil Taylor has gone to them. He is the only person I know who has gone to them.

Q   When was the Albanian Society founded?

DAVE   I think it was founded by A. L. Lloyd, and I think Bill Bland was energetically involved from its early stages. Could be around mid-seventies. I have to look at it. It was when Albania recognised different Marxist-Leninist parties, sometimes back in 1977-78. It was the time when Albania broke with China, but that was the time when British Marxist-Leninist parties broke with China. Not all parties broke with China. Reg Birch didn't break with China, and I think they even became pro-Russian after this. It's all mixed up these days. I had a thing recently, where I discovered that Marxist-Leninist Party, which Cornelius Cardew was involved in, and the musicians that I know, still seem to support China. This is a case in thinking, I suspect, my enemy's enemy is my friend. So, the enemy is still America. If you ask me, they're all imperialists.

Q   That was the theory of Enver Hoxha.

DAVE   I think that's probably right!

Q   When visiting Albania in the '70s, were you involved in the party's activities? How was the Albanian Society connected to the RCPB ML?

DAVE   The Albanian Society was not tied to any party. In fact, it made a big thing of being completely independent, in order to attract non-political people, or people who had other interests in Albania. Although, everyone knew Bill Bland was who he was, and his rankings. Though he made sure that the Party didn't take the Society over, neither did the party want . . to take it over anyway. Although, obviously quite few of them showed interest in it, and supported it. But they respected the line that it shouldn't be a party organisation. So, yes, the Society was non-political.

Q   It was not political, but it was quite supportive of the socialist line of Albania, at least that is the impression I got from reading *Albanian Life* journals.

DAVE   Of course, but dissenting letters were published. The people who wrote for it tended to know more about the country than those who didn't. Those who knew about the country, would be attracted if not by politics, at least by the independent line which was taken, and would respect that. Thinking of the people who wrote about it. Bill Bland wrote a lot in the journal.

Q   Could you tell more who Bill Bland was?

DAVE   I don't know if I sent you earlier, Bland wrote a big article on religion in Albania. It is a very interesting article, and it is a very good example of how his mind works. In other words, he is not going to accept everything told by whoever. He is a theorist. One of his differences, presumably, with the Revolutionary Communist Party of Britain Marxist-Leninist was he thought that they are theoretically weak. I think he was probably right. Also, I think he was always ahead of the game. In 1951 the Communist Party of Great Britain, as it was called back then, came up with the idea of British Road to Socialism. He and two other people left the Party because of that. He claimed it was a revisionist idea. Bill Bland was a bloke seeing revisionism in every corner. Because he was so theoretically strong and reasoned, he tended to have a full independent line, and he didn't mind whom he offended by doing that. He and two other people, whom he hadn't met, left the Party. He was active in New Zealand. There is an interview with him done in the nineties, telling all this. In 1964 he wrote an article which criticised Mao. That was not a thing done that time... He spent some time learning Albanian. He couldn't speak Albanian, but he read it perfectly. I found this very strange indeed, because Albanian is one of these languages which is spoken the way it is written. It's not like English, which is the worst language like that. Apparently he read and translated things perfectly.

Q   I read his book *Tangled Web*, which he co-authored with Ian Price. It is rigorous and serious research. Reading it made me wonder why so many leftist people from Britain were involved with the socialist project of Albania. Maybe Albania was an unresolved question to the British people, with the Corfu incident and the gold scandal. Due to this reason, I thought that perhaps through their interest in Albania, the British people were channelling their criticism to their own imperialist-nationalist politics. Do you agree with this?

DAVE   I think the interest in Albania goes back to the 1960s, when it was seen, as I said earlier, as a strange European country. Probably the exoticism of that idea. People didn't know anything about it. I think most people knew nothing about the gold, or the Corfu Channel incident, unless they read the books. Not many people have read the books. And the Corfu Channel incident was not discussed in mainstream media until the 1990s. Because it was not viewed as particularly important... it was viewed as being off the edge of the world. Don't forget that we didn't have diplomatic relations with Albania. Britain has diplomatic relations with everybody, apart from Albania, Guatemala, for years and years, because of Belize, Cambodia, and North Korea. There were countries we were occasionally disagreeing with, like Uganda under Idi Amin. Otherwise, we had diplomatic relations with every country in Europe, apart from Albania.

    There were good reasons nobody would not know much about Albania, and probably different people would be attracted for different reasons. Therefore Bland was attracted purely by the politics; Ian Price by the music and dance. He was interested in music and dance, he has a group playing Albanian music, and others playing Bulgarian and Turkish. He played a lot of instruments. This is where he came to be interested in Albania. ... As I said with Regent Holidays you could visit Albania with groups. Probably about 20 people in each group. There would be one or two guides for each group, looking after us. These tourist groups included some interesting people: there was a fair proportion of people who've been everywhere else in Europe except in Albania, so they were actually ticking Albania off the list. Quite few people had an angle, the reason; they would not just sit on the beach. I went to Albania in 1987 and 1988 with the group called Skanderbeg Reisen, which was based in Vienna, an Austrian version of... Regent Holidays. With them you could stay a month. So in 1987 I stayed for a month. Quite a few who went with that group would sit on the beach as you can guess. Austria does not have . . . sea, and Albania has pretty much the nearest and cheapest. But in English groups, just everybody who went had an angle.

Q I think in the seventies and the eighties, even if you were affirmative to what was going on in Albania, it was already a political stance. Because almost everyone else in the world was against Albania. People think that the whole country was under a totalitarian dictatorship, run by the ruthless autocrat, etc. that there is nothing positive in the country. Your story is particularly interesting because you've seen something behind all this propaganda machinery going on against Albania.

DAVE I think quite a lot of people saw what was going on in Albania when they went there. As I said before people didn't go to Albania just for beach time. Being there they would find out about the politics, because guides would not only talk about the history of the places we would visit, but they would also talk about what people are doing, and why they are doing, what party does not like, what is the party's opinion, and all that, also about actual things. People would also ask things, and guides had to answer those questions. You would not be able to ignore the discussions that were going on.

Q Could you share more about your visits to Albania? You were collecting music, meeting musicians, and doing lots of research there.

DAVE It was difficult to do research in the summer. In July or August, when we usually would go to Albania, there would be no concerts happening.
I found out about the music by recording from the radio. I had to go a few times before I actually met any musicians, apart from young lads who were playing in bands in the Durrës tourist zone. Also what I did was that whenever we arrived in town, I would go to the bookshop and buy anything on music, a lot of musical scores, in Albanian obviously, so, I would find out about things in that way. After I composed *Albanian Summer*, A.L. Lloyd (around 1982) gave me a letter of invitation to the Institute of People's Culture. That is when I went there. That was the official visit, if you like. I think the guide who went with me happened to be the most experienced guide, a bloke who was highly respected. His name was Edi Kurtezi. There was a composer called Tish Daia, a bloke who ran the Institute was called Mustafa Gërcaliu, he was not a musician, and there I also met Ferial Daja, a female ethnomusicologist. In my following trips I went back there. Once because I arranged it. Through Tish Daia, I met other composers, like Feim Ibrahimi. Usually all went very well with guides organising meetings there. I remember one year I got pissed off with the guide, and went by myself. I just turned up there. All went fine. In the evening when the guide asked what I had done today, I just told I went to the Institute. He was very embarrassed, because he should have organised it.

Q So, normally everything was very well organised, right?

DAVE Usually, yes. Sometimes the same guides turned up again and again. Like this Edi Kurtezi, he was my guide in 1973, but he was also my guide a couple of times later. Things went easy with him. But if it was a young guy, things would have been a bit difficult. This is how it was. It didn't go much further from that. I didn't hear any concerts where Albanian compositions were played. That never happened. I never went to the Gjirokastra folk music festival.

Q	You're mentioning A. L. Lloyd now. I got the impression that he was an important figure in introducing Albanian music to Britain?
DAVE	That's right. He was the only person.
Q	Could you tell a bit more about him? Did you met him?
DAVE	Well, he was the president of the Albanian Society.
Q	So, he wasn't a member of CPGB ML?
DAVE	No, he wasn't. He was a member of the Communist Party of Great Britain. He was an old folk musician, and these guys are left wing. He had a considerable reputation as a folk music specialist. He was in Albania several times, and he was happy to be the president of the Albanian Society, which was more of an honorary position. The president was not who ran the society. Bland was the secretary. Lloyd, who was president, was not organising things. It was Bland. It was slightly like the Communist Party, where the secretary was the most important. Lloyd was a very respected person. (Kurtezi guided him as well.) I didn't know him so well, but he sent me a couple of recommendation letters, and I met him a couple of times. I told him about the Albanian Summer composition, and he introduced me to people we met in the Society meetings.
Q	How did you decide to compose the *Albanian Summer* album?
DAVE	You have to ask that to Jan Steele?
Q	I asked him. He told me he got a grant and commissioned you to write a piece for his repertoire.
DAVE	Yes. Jan is very a go-ahead. He gets things done, he's energetic. Not like me. He is very skilful, he plays the saxophone and flute, but he is very skilful in other kinds of music as well. He was not only good with Western kind of music, he played Indian pop music, jazz, and reggae. His father was a communist, a union leader in Birmingham. Jan is the left wing, but he never was tied to any political party. Probably, he learned very early that these guys are confused; one day you like Stalin, and other day you hate him. Because he was growing up with all this.
Q	Were you a member of the party?
DAVE	No. I was just a supporter of the Marxist-Leninist Party. Basically, a sympathiser. Not a party liner.
Q	I am curious to know how you were connecting the involvement in experimental music with Albanian music, which was very conventional and traditional? You were at the same time involved in the Scratch Orchestra and doing experimental music, but as well writing about Albanian classical music and defending the socialist-realist form in there? How were you able to connect these two?
DAVE	Ha! Good question. I don't think I particularly connected them. But musically Albania was a special case. Before the Second World War, effectively there was no composed music. Their first ballet, 1963, by Tish Daija; Çesk Zadeja, 1956, the first symphony. All these things happened in the fifties and the sixties. Albanian composers basically had to work from the scratch. They had to start from zero.
	Eventually some of the composers born in the twenties went to study abroad. Tish Daija said to me proudly that his graduation form was signed by Shostakovich. He studied in Moscow. Feim Ibrahimi who was born in 1935 was the first composer not to study abroad. He studied in Tirana. That would've been the end of the fifties. Most of them before that studied in

Moscow, at least until 1961. After that they all had to come back, which is why Feim Ibrahimi was the first home grown composer. So anyway, the reason I was supportive was that I was impressed with how far Albanian composers have gotten in the years since the war. Especially considering the fact that they did not know much about . . . recent developments, avant-garde music included. On the other hand, there were certain modernist composers who were permissible, like Bartók or Prokofiev. Bartók because his music was influenced by folk music, and Prokofiev being the Soviet composer, but both of them wrote some music which were extremely dissonant, I am not sure though how much they heard of that in Albania. In fact, Albanian musicians were not afraid of dissonance; some of them used it for sarcastic purposes. For example, there is a piece by Feim Ibrahimi, written in Geg dialect, 'Tan' Shqipnia asht betue pa gjak malet mos me i Ishue' (1978), which is pretty dissonant.

Albanian music is incredibly romantic, very passionate, especially the orchestral stuff. The standard of some instrumental players was pretty amazing. Not all instruments in general, but violinists in particular. It must be because of the folk music, which was very important there. You go to a conservatory, they ask you to play folk music as well as Mozart or Beethoven. It was perhaps that simplistic reason that I was mostly attracted to orchestral music featuring the violin. I am not a big fan of . . . opera. I can't stand the singing. Their opera seemed a little bit alien to me. Also, I didn't find much interesting piano music in Albania, which is for me a very important instrument.

So, the most amazing thing was that the country without the tradition could go so far, in such a short time. This must have happened in other countries as well, but not in the twentieth century. Perhaps similar things happened in the twentieth century outside of Europe, yes, but not in Europe. But no country started from scratch as Albania did. Given that Albanians were not encouraged to study modernist music. You have this special situation; you have the country which had to start from scratch after the Second World War, and where the modernist tendencies were effectively denied. So what do they do? It's a unique situation. Just as Albania is a unique country. So, I was interested to know what they came with. Of course, most of the stuff is pretty ordinary, pretty amateurish, but some of it isn't. Those I mentioned, I rank very highly. But not all. Çesk Zadeja, for example, one of the kingpins of Albanian music, but never really liked his music very much. As a composer he had a very high reputation, but I didn't really get it. Whereas Ibrahimi was a composer closer to modernism, in the sense he used . . . dissonance to emphasise the passionate, because most Albanian music is very passionate. They don't write long pieces. You have to write short pieces, therefore they are very concentrated, and very passionate, and everything happens in a very small space.

Q   It seems that you were impressed by the spirit of Albanian music, which began from scratch, from zero. Were you enthusiastic only about classical music? What about folk music? Was it undergoing any big change or invention? You wrote an article about the work of the Institute of People's Culture. I remember that you described how busy and organised they were.

DAVE   Of course, folk music is different from classical music. Folk music was happening before the war. I got recordings of Albanian music from the twenties. Some of it's pretty much the same, in terms of the traditions being kept. One of the good things which the regime in Albania did was to encourage that. Folk music is incidentally fascinating because the north and south are very different. The countryside and the town are very different. The town music is Turkish influenced, the country music isn't. The Geg music is different from the Tosk music, and all within the country which is the size of Wales. Well I have a lot of cassettes, tons of them, and it's all very varied. I don't tire of listening to them at all.

Q Recordings from Radio Tirana?

DAVE Yes. Almost all from the radio, recorded while I was there in Albania.

Q So, when you were sending all these recorded cassettes back to the UK, did you have any problems at the borders? I am making this question, having heard about the vigilance of the country of Albania and how they monitor and control, especially people from abroad.

DAVE No. I had problems with Yugoslavs who were interested in literature. Especially in the seventies. They didn't allow works of Enver Hoxha or anything else from Albania.

Q What about when you were entering Albania?

DAVE No problem in that. You could take whatever you want inside. There were only two things when entering Albania. One was, the hair was too long. They were also interested in what newspapers you had. Quite often things were confiscated. But always returned to you when you would leave back. I give you an example of my visit in 1977. I had two books with me. One was called *The Necessity of Art* by Ernst Fischer, and I had a book entitled *Experimental Music* by an English composer Michael Nyman. This book happened to open at a photo of a mate of mine (John Tilbury) tied up with ropes and trying to play despite that. But they confiscated *The Necessity of Art*, because it was written by an East German, presumably. Experimental music, very good, fine, but not the necessity of art (laughing). Though I got the book back when I left. People couldn't take the *Times* newspaper in for example, it was all a bit arbitrary. But the last few times when I went I flew to Rinas, and I don't remember them bothering at all what I had with me, at the customs.

Q But there was no problem when you were leaving with all these recorded cassettes?

DAVE No problem, no problem.

Q Your story is a bit different from the usual ones.

DAVE The printed word is subversive, the sound and cassettes aren't. I don't know, I haven't thought about it. The books or scores I would post from Albania.

Q Going back to the *Albanian Summer*. What was your idea with this composition? It sounds eclectic. When I asked Jan how he'd describe the album, he defined it as picaresque. Was this album an intention to have an overview of Albanian music?

DAVE I think the idea was to celebrate Albanian music. One of the contributory factors was Jan Steele himself. I knew what kind of player he was. I met him a long time before that, and I knew what kind of music he did. He was a free improviser in those days. His method of improvisation was, I believe, influenced by A. L. Lloyd record. I haven't thought about it for years.

	But I remember he told me once that he got a lot of inspiration from A. L. Lloyd's Albanian record. That is why perhaps I thought that I could write some Albanian music for Jan. The thing about that piece is that it's very long, and it's ordered in a rather random way. I would never write a piece like that, again. And one of my misgivings about it is that is too close to the model.
Q	Do you want to say that the final result is too close to the source of inspiration?
DAVE	It is a pastiche. It is too similar. I have misgivings on that score. On the other hand, I voiced this misgiving to Steve Beresford, who is an improviser here, who's been very supportive of the piece, and he said that that is why he really likes it. It's quite an uncultivated approach. There are quite a few improvisers who seem to like it a lot. But also I find that the piece . . . a bit of a mish-mash. If I wrote longer pieces since then, they would be much more cohesive. Do you understand?
Q	I think so.
DAVE	It should have made much more sense as the whole thing. Whereas in *Albanian Summer* what happens is that you get one section, then another section; it's not often apparent how sections marry up against each other.
Q	I thought that was your initial aim, to have it as an episodic structure?
DAVE	In a way, I did. That's right. But I am not sure if I succeeded in doing a thing which makes sense as a whole. Perhaps that doesn't matter.
Q	Yes, the album is really good.
DAVE	There are some parts that I find really embarrassing. That is over-passionate. This is not Albanian at all. I mean the passion would be Albanian, but it is the kind of music which comes from the big country.
Q	Kind of German leftist music.
DAVE	Little bit like Hans Eisler maybe.
Q	Did you do any other composition around Albanian themes?
DAVE	Yes. There is one piece in particular, called *Alban Lament*.
Q	There's some singing in there.
DAVE	The singing has nothing to do with Albanian. I took all the meanings of Alban, which I could think of. Alba is another word for Scotland. Alba is also the dawn in different languages. The voice is actually a slow-down singing of Scottish music, slow-down bagpipe music. It has the use of Albanian music as well, as you could hear. There are four *kabas* happening simultaneously at one point.
Q	In his biography of Cardew, Tilbury mentions that in the mid-seventies, you were already doing arrangements of Albanian music for Cardew.
DAVE	Early seventies, actually. I think I did a few of these arrangements before I actually went to Albania. But there was one tune that I really liked. Though, I never actually find out who really wrote it. It was a song called 'To Heroic Vietnam', which Cornelius used a bit of . . . for a piece he wrote called 'Vietnam Sonata' and he asked me to write a small section of it using this Albanian tune. It was in the record of Albanian partisan songs, which I bought before I went to Albania. After I heard this live in Saranda in 1973. Obviously it was a known song then in Albania.
Q	How do you approach writing political music?
DAVE	There are a lot of ways for composers to deal with that. There are composers who write some modernist avant-garde music, and add

a political element. That doesn't always seem to make sense to me. There's no problem in doing experimental things with music, if that makes sense in context. I will give you a simple example. I have written a piece in support of Palestinian Intifada in 1999. What that piece has is that I hit the piano. You might think this is rather an unusual, modernist thing to do. (It's actually not so modernist, people have been using this sort of things for a hundred years.) Anyway, it seems an unlike technique to use, but I used it in that piece. I wanted to give an impression of Arabic drumming that doesn't seem an obvious thing to do with a piano. In terms of playing that to any audience, it can be intimidating to hit the piano like that. Though, nobody said to me this is a strange thing. Because it fits in the piece. It fits in the background.

Q Do you imply that even the modernist, or experimental music has to correspond to the context?

DAVE The way I write political music is quite often using actual songs. There are many composers, whom when you hear you would not recognize the actual song, because they destroyed it so much. The way I do the arrangements of songs is to actually take the song away from what it originally sounded like, but the tune always would be there. And I try to do something relevant in terms of having some elements of folk music recognized as such. Now, this very much sounds like a socialist-realist line [laughing], though it's not intended to be that. I just thought that was the most sensible thing to do in those circumstances.

Q You mentioned earlier, that the misgivings of *Albanian Summer* are that it resembles its source; it is similar to folk elements it deals with. Back then, was your initial idea to do a modernist piece and not a political one?

DAVE I am speaking as a composer. It is a technical thing. I am saying that, in *Albanian Summer* I didn't digest the music properly. That's the word. I haven't digested it. The music is still in my mouth. That aspect is what bothers me. I am quite happy to live with that, but I am not going to write a piece like that. I would now more likely use Albanian materials which would not sound at all like Albanian. For example there is a central Albanian rhythm, a very interesting rhythm, which sounds in seven. The bits are in different lengths. They sound as if they are drunk. It is called 'aksak', it's in Turkish. It means limping. In fact, A.L. Lloyd wrote an article on aksak rhythm. It is the kind of rhythm you'll get in Bulgaria, Greece, Turkey, Romania, and Albania. There are plenty of its uses in Albania. Musicologists seem quite puzzled about it. It is an unpredictable kind of rhythm. I am using it quite a lot in my music, but they don't sound like Albanian.

Q I want to go back to politics. Were you reading Enver Hoxha?

DAVE Yes, I got all of his books. I haven't read them for years and years. But, yes.

Q Were you reading these discussions about Beethoven and music in that context?

DAVE I think the thing about Beethoven that's mostly to do with China, and that's the big difference between Albania and China in the early seventies. China had a Cultural Revolution and so any music which was produced was Peking Opera kind of thing. You wouldn't hear other stuff. In Albania there seemed to be a situation where the music was produced, and was encouraged. Every town in Albania had an orchestra. The folk music was as varied as it was. Culturally it did not seem to be much of a problem there,

	in other words, there were a lot of people keen to make music and publish it. I thought that was very healthy.
Q	Were your own political views close to the line of the Party of Labour of Albania? Were you finding their discussions relevant?
DAVE	I think a lot of people accepted things because they were naive. The picture that they achieved a lot of things was generally accepted; but we did not ask at what cost. We didn't ask that question. Some of the politics was too hard, but the general stance was one of which I agreed with. They sort of basically coincided with my own views. I thought some of the stuff was wrong, for example the ban on religion. Also Bland was critical of it. On the other hand, I did enjoy the Atheist Museum in Shkodra.
Q	Could you tell a bit more about it?
DAVE	It was fantastic. One of the most controversial parts of the visit. It had a record of various paintings. I remember a huge painting of the Pope, with some graffitti underneath. Basically, anti-religious paintings. The person who ran it was a wonderful personality, very jovial. He was able to deal with any kind of questions. No problems at all. I'm afraid it does not exist anymore.
Q	Was your last visit to Albania in 1990?
DAVE	Yes, I haven't been since then.
Q	So, you have no idea what happened after communism.
DAVE	No! Except what I read about it. I haven't been there since, which is a great regret. Well, my life changed quite a bit at the same time, in 1991, and so forth. I know there would be nothing similar to what I am used to. I would like to go to places I haven't been. As a tourist you never get anywhere near Bajram Curri, or to Përmet, I never went to Peshkopi. You asked me earlier about my impressions of how things changed in Albania. Well, I remember that during the 1977 visit, the authorities were most vigilant, because they felt very unsafe, because they just split with China. I think everybody knew this before it even happened; this is an impression I got. So, people were very careful. In the seventies, for example, there was no visits to Vlora. The reason given was there it was a military installation. In the eighties it was no problem to visit Vlora. I could say that they were a bit more paranoid in the seventies.
Q	What about 1985, after Hoxha's death; did you sense any changes?
DAVE	Not particularly. The death of Hoxha was an isolated instance. On the other hand, it was unusual. I don't think people got more friendly after that. They were friendly anyway. Perhaps more people seemed to be more open. Or maybe I just knew the place better, and therefore knew how to approach the people better. My very impression is that nothing has really changed. They were just getting a bit more up to date. That might be because of the trade that was going on, the trade with some strange places. In the late eighties there were more things in the shops.
Q	Were you visiting factories?
DAVE	Yes. Some were more interesting than others. Copper wire factory in Shkodra was the one which was always on the programme. Not a very interesting one at all.
Q	Going back to music; you were a member of the People's Liberation Music (PLM) and Progressive Culture Association (PCA) in the seventies in England.

DAVE   PCA was something to do with Marxist-Leninist party. PLM didn't start with the party but it gradually moved into a party organisation. Tilbury was one of the first members. It was started by a bloke called Laurie Scott Baker. They did songs which Baker wrote, and gradually Cardew took it from Tilbury, because he was busy with doing concerts. I was only involved in it for a year or so. I played the French horn, and did a few backing vocals. They had quite a good female singer, called Vicky Silver. Some of the songs were good, some not. In a rock music sense it was very straight. Cornelius insisted on having 'questions and answers' during the intervals between concerts. Cornelius was very keen in questioning and interrogating the audience, which was not always a good idea, as you can imagine. On the other hand, PCA was basically the people who were party people, not the same people from PLM. They were interested in getting people's songs sung, and PCA was the banner under which that tended to happen: people singing songs.

Q   Was the same musical repertoire of PCA the same as in PLM?

DAVE   No. It wasn't. PLM would do rock songs which were probably written by Laurie Baker, or someone else. Cardew wrote a couple of rock songs. Whereas PCA was a bit like having a small choir and a few instruments. They would sing old revolutionary songs, not necessarily in a rock manner. The organisations were actually quite different. Although, maybe, PLM became subsumed in PCA. I never knew what happened to PCA in the end. I didn't have very much to do with it, really. Just occasionally played with them. There might be a meeting where I would be involved. There was a meeting about Lenin, and so there was a song done by Hans Eisler called Lenin. We would play that, for example. At the party meeting it would be said that it was done by PCA, in other words PCA was umbrella terms to cover that. PLM was a rock music, which functioned separately from the party.

Q   You were also a member of the Scratch Orchestra?

DAVE   Yes. I was active with Scratch Orchestra in 1971, 72, and 73. Orchestra has been going on since 1969. I didn't come to London until 1971, not before Discontent Meetings. So, in the Summer of 1971, there were various so-called Discontent Meetings in the Scratch Orchestra, which were basically discussions about what was wrong in what the Scratch Orchestra was doing. In other words, they were beginning to realise that they wanted to do one thing, but in effect they were doing another. They were trying to live outside of the system, but in reality they were asking for money from the system. Most people in the Scratch Orchestra were interested in doing experimental stuff, which meant social inquiry. Therefore it wasn't so surprising to me that suddenly they got into politics. It seemed to me an extension of what it was all about. Even the kind of music and performances they were doing, avant-garde or experimental, whatever word you like to use, but actually what people were thinking, and that was down to Tilbury and Keith Rowe, who left the discussion in one of the discontents meetings criticising the Scratch Orchestra from the Marxist point of view. That was the discussion, which was most telling, and had the most influence. The political awareness of the Scratch Orchestra came from that moment. From the next year, which is when I joined, there were a lot of the old Scratch activities going on, but also a lot of political discussions going on, singing political songs as well. So, the two were side by side.

	I joined at the beginning of the change, but the change took at least a year, two years actually.
Q	Which of these sides pulled you towards the Scratch Orchestra?
DAVE	I read about the SO musical activities in London, when I was in Birmingham, and I thought that London is where I want to be. I came down to London to see the Scratch performance. It had nothing to do with improvisation. It was two pieces by Cornelius Cardew from *The Great Learning*. Each of the paragraphs from the Great Learning, which lasts quite a long time. It was a concert which involved Paragraph 1 and Paragraph 4, both lasting about an hour. Both of those were consistent, well behaved, and organised activity, then they did in some of their anarchist times. Because, quite a lot of the time, the Scratch Orchestra put on some anarchist type of performances, which anything could happen, and did. Whereas these pieces by Cardew gave you a way of getting from the beginning to the end. I was very impressed by it, and thought that this is the kind of music I want to be trying. So, no, it wasn't to do with politics, to begin with. Nor, really was for anyone else in the Scratch Orchestra. They didn't join it because of political reasons.
Q	I guess Cardew was not so political at that time?
DAVE	No, he became political during 1971.
Q	During the Discontent Meetings?
DAVE	Well, after. Tilbury and Rowe created a lot of discussion. Various people went along with it, various didn't. Eventually, pretty much everybody who was not interested in politics, or disproved the politics, left. By which time the Scratch Orchestra changed completely anyway.

MUSIC IN ALBANIA
by Dave Smith

The wealth and variety of music in Albania is astonishing, considering that the country has just over 2 ¾ million people inhabiting an area slightly larger (and even more mountainous) than Wales. Singing appears to be a national sport even more popular than football — hardly surprising, perhaps, since a visit to a kindergarten revealed that even young children are able to perform songs and recite poetry with both a remarkable confidence and a surprising lack of self-consciousness.

The three-to-five-piece bands that play in bars, restaurants and hotels (there are no juke-boxes) often include a virtuoso instrumentalist, usually a clarinettist or a violinist: technical dexterity, full-blooded tone quality intricate ornamentation, and frequent glissandi (and sometimes bewildering rhythmic groupings) all contribute to the cheerful rhapsodic nature of their performance. This sort of band, known as a *saze*, also includes instruments such as piano accordion, guitar (possibly electric), and drum-kit, and is typical of urban popular music, forms of which developed during the 500-year Turkish occupation. Despite certain oriental features, it sounds just as peculiarly Albanian (rather than all-purpose Balkan) as the strikingly different rural folk music. This itself displays considerable regional differences, particularly the vocal music, which tends towards a hard-edged, nasal homophony in the north and a complex, drone-based, ancient-sounding polyphony in the south, where probably more types of part-singing have developed than in any other region of Europe. Instrumental folk ensembles frequently feature long-necked lutes and shepherds' pipes. Lutes often accompany songs, but instruments such as pipes (*fyell* and *kavall*) and the small double clarinet (*zumare*) can sometimes be heard to best advantage when they are played alone;[1] customarily employing circular breathing, soloists on these instruments improvise "pieces" based on frequent and varied repetition of simple motifs. A counterpart in urban music (and one of its highlights) is the *kaba*,

> ...an instrumental improvisation of vast territorial extent;...as with the Blues in the USA, every performance of the *kaba* is achingly familiar yet always fresh and different.[2]

Bands that are used to performing for tourists will often play Western tunes as well, complete with Albanian-style expression and ornamentation; they seem to have a peculiar affinity for tangos and soulful popular numbers — "Petite Fleur" and "House of the Rising Sun" are particular favourites.

Albanian folk music, then, is a strong cultural force which is very much alive and well. The folk music archive of the Institute of People's Culture in Tirana holds about 21,000 folk melodies. "This may seem a large collection", the assistant director told me, "but it is small in comparison to what we must have". There are frequent national and regional contests and festivals, of which the most celebrated is the National Folklore Festival, held in

Gjirokastra, a picturesque city renowned for its unique architecture. This festival is held every five years, most recently in October 1978.

Thanks to the pioneering work of the late A. L. Lloyd, Albanian folk music is not completely unknown in Britain. But what of the music produced by Albanian composers? John Jansson's performance of Çesk Zadeja's "Toccata" at the *Albanian Society*'s memorial meeting for A. L. Lloyd in January was possibly the first British performance of any Albanian composition. But however little known these composers may be to the rest of the world, they seem well publicised and widely appreciated within their own country. Armed with a radio-cassette machine and a daily newspaper, I was able to record a fairly representative sample of orchestral, choral and operatic music, though solo piano and chamber music proved more difficult to locate.

A general guide-book informed me that Albanian composers base themselves on the folklore of the country and avoid

> ...abstract and decadent trends. Their aesthetic aim is 'national in form and socialist in substance', as the basic principle of socialist realism.[3]

I expected to hear music that was heavily dependent on nationalist composers of the 19th. and early 20th. centuries and Soviet socialist realist composers of the Stalin era. These expectations were fuelled by the knowledge that the conditions created by the Turkish occupation, the ravages of two world wars and the inter-war repressive dictatorship of King Zog made it impossible for composers to flourish. In the immediate post-war years, they virtually had to start from scratch. Consequently the first Albanian operetta, "Agimi" (The Dawn) by Kristo Kono, appeared as late as 1953, the first opera, "Mrika" by Preng Jakova, in 1958, and the first ballet "Halili dhe Hajrija" (Halil and Hajrija) by Tish Daia, in 1963.

My first reactions to much of what I heard were mixed. Many pieces were attractively tuneful, spirited, and cheerful, and all were tonal (in the broadest sense). But often I was left feeling rather bewildered by what seemed to be a strange attitude to harmonic progression, or a rate of change of ideas considerably faster than, say, Poulenc's Sokol Shupo's "Rhapsody for Piano and Orchestra" was a particularly inscrutable example. Perhaps the most disorientating thing was that it was often difficult to relate these works to Western models. I heard only one piece — Lorenc Antoni's "Pjesë për malësorët" (Piece for Highlanders) — that could be accused of a particularly strong indebtedness (to Dvořák); the expected whiffs of Bartók and Prokofiev were rare, though a vaguely Russian-sounding orchestral palette was in evidence at times.

The main radio station, Radio Tirana, often presents programmes consisting entirely of rhapsodies, symphonic poems, suites, ballet music or even overtures. One composer whose music was broadcast frequently and instantly appealed to me was Aleksandër Peçi (born 1951). His attractive

"Rhapsody for Violin and Orchestra" (1977) is typical: subtitled "Valle e jone, valle e popullit" ("Our dance, dance of the people", it reflects the composer's contact with the folk music of the south, particularly that of Përmet, a town near the Greek border, the music of which is noted for its lyrical warmth and lively character. Peçi's "Rhapsody" contrasts these two types of material — he introduces an authentic lyrical folk-tune at one point — before launching into a brief but astonishing cadenza, related to the particular variety of *kaba* found in Përmet and featuring a stylised "wailing" figure and retuning of the violin's G string.

This is a good example of a work that openly displays its folk music connections without sounding like a sophisticated arrangement. While it is unmistakably of the 20th. century, it is light years away from, say, Bartók or Enescu, being pretty consonant and full of typically Romantic gestures. The clarity and immediate attractiveness reappeared in other works by Peçi for solo instrument and orchestra, particularly the "Cello Fantasia" (1979). The "Variations for Horn" (1975) is a less memorable piece (I've never heard a horn player use so much vibrato), but the suite for piano and orchestra entitled "Kuadro heroizmit" (Pictures of Heroism) is more dissonant and highly charged and contains flourishes reminiscent of Prokofiev. "Pjesë për flaut" (Piece for Flute), accompanied by an almost Latin American-sounding folk orchestra, is unashamedly "light" in character and reflects the fact that Peçi, like most other Albanian composers, is equally at ease writing film music, a stirring revolutionary song, or even "light music".[4]

Not all composers make such clear reference to folk music as Peçi. Several seem to favour highly impassioned minor-key tensions, which are effective in disguising folk sources, or so it would appear. One piece that uses such techniques is "Rhapsody No. 1 for Orchestra" (1973) by Feim Ibrahimi (b. 1937); a useful little book on Albanian composers, which I managed to pick up, assured me that this work

> ...directly evokes authentic folk rhapsodies[5]

Much as I admired the work for its emotional drama and struggle, I couldn't detect a very strong folk connection. Most Western listeners, I imagine, would happily sit through the symphonic poems "Atdheu" (Motherland, 1974) by Shpëtim Kushta (b. 1946) and "Borova" by Thoma Gaqi (b. 1948) without being aware of any folk reference whatsoever. Solemnity and epic-heroics permeate the first of these, while "Borova" (named after a village the inhabitants of which were massacred by the Nazis) is suitably imbued with tragedy and a reflection of the courage of the people who struggled against the invaders.

The orchestration of these symphonic poems is predominantly dark-coloured, a feature common to much Albanian music. Peçi's music is more transparently textured than most, but that of Tish Daia (b. 1926) is the most individual sounding. Daia's "Rhapsody for Flute and Orchestra" (1981) is a short but effective essay in highly ornamented, lyrical-pastoral, low-register flute writing, which passes quickly and effortlessly into impassioned orchestral tuttis. The string writing is particularly imaginative, ranging from beefy arpeggio figures (reminiscent of Janaček) in the tuttis to quiet glassy-textured accompaniment in the early stages of the work. Effective string writing is also a feature of an excerpt I heard from a much earlier work "Halili dhe Hajrija" (1961-2). The events portrayed in this, the first Albanian ballet, occurred in the 18th. century, when Turkish oppression encountered the resistance of the highland warriors. Musically the piece furnishes further evidence of Daia's ability to cope with rapid contrast without creating the feeling that the composer is presenting too much information — in fact, Daia's ideas seem to flow at a more relaxed rate than those of most of his compatriots.

"Halili dhe Hajrija" was performed 150 times between 1963 and 1973, which is some measure of its popularity. Encouraged by its success, several other ballets appeared in the 1960s, such as "Delina" by (Çesk Zadeja (b. 1927), "Fatosi partizan" (The Boy Partisan) by Kozma Laro, and "Cuca e maleve" (The Girl from the Mountains) by Nikolla Zoraqi (b. 1929). Scene 2 of Act 2 of Zoraqi's ballet, which was one of the most impressive things I heard during my stay, seems to indicate that the composer's forte is the broadly lyrical and the feverishly passionate; the extraordinarily jolly "Uvertura festive" (Festival Overture) (1969) is barely recognisable as a work by the same composer. I also managed to buy a piano reduction of Zoraqi's "Third Violin Concerto", which looks fiendishly difficult but, judging by Ibrahim Mali's dazzling performance of Peçi's Rhapsody, there are violinists able to cope with it.

One of the most prolific composers appears to be Tonin Harapi (b. 1928), whose work seems fairly diatonic in comparison with that of most of his countrymen. His suite "Vullnetarët" (The Volunteers) (1965) is a vocal suite dedicated to the youth of the country, whose voluntary work on such projects as the construction of the railways is well known; it is a cheerful and energetic three-movement choral piece, which pays tribute to this topical phenomenon. Harapi seems less attracted to the kind of impassioned utterance common to the works of Ibrahimi, Zoraqi and Kushta, even in dramatic works such as his opera "Zgjimi" (The Awakening) (1974). His relatively lightweight "Second Rhapsody for Piano and Orchestra" (a work that makes obvious allusions to folk music) seems to bear this out.

I should have liked to hear more of the operatic achievements of Albania's senior composers Preng Jakova (1919 - 69) and Kristo Kono (b. 1907), both of whom are accredited People's Artists (the others are Tish Daia, Çesk Zadeja and Avni Mula, while several more are Artists of Merit). Kono's opera "Lulja e kujtimit" (The Flower of Remembrance) (1958) has a marvellously rousing martial finale, which sounds like the result of a collaboration between Verdi and Eisler.

I was disappointed in the small piano pieces I occasionally, came across. The brief "Toccata" of Çesk Zadeja seems less effective in terms of the piano than does his "Symphonic Suite" in terms of the orchestra.

The toccata-type piece, often involving fast semi-quavers in alternate hands, is a popular choice since there is a natural counterpart in the fast virtuouso playing of the çifteli, a two-string lute.

The position of Albania in the world of composition is quite a peculiar one. Here is a body of music in which the element of communication is of paramount importance. Quite frankly, it was refreshing to hear a large amount of recently composed tonal music, little of which struck me as being trite or ill-considered. Composers have flourished for barely 40 years in Albania, and yet their music ignores almost all the fashionable tendencies in Western music from Schoenberg and Stravinsky onwards (though Albanian higher musical education includes study of such phenomena). Their reasons for this lie in a popular political stance, which maintains that

> ...the efforts of the present-day reactionary aesthetes to advertise a 'universal' art serve the interest of the imperialist bourgeoisie, which has always striven to denigrate or to eliminate the cultural traditions of smaller nations and the national spirit in art and culture, to facilitate its cultural aggression and the subjugation of nations... starting from impressionism and expressionism (and continuing) to the present dodecaphonic, serial and punctualistic music ... they all try to justify themselves under the cloak of 'innovation', the 'search for the new' at all costs, while breaking down every connection with the best progressive traditions of the peoples and, above all, seeking to divert attention from the essential problems of the content, from the major questions that are concerning mankind today, the working class, the youth, the peoples of the world who are fighting for their liberation and their social rights. [6]

— *Albanian Life*, no. 26, 1983

NOTES

1. A record that features solos from different instruments is "Folklore instrumental albanais" (Vendemiaire VDE 114, AD 37). Two other records that I can recommend are "L'Albanie folklorique" (Disques Cellier 010) and "Folk Music of Albania", collected and edited by A. L. Lloyd (Topic 12T 154).
2. A. L. Lloyd: Sleeve notes to "Folk Music of Albania".
3. "An Outline of the People's Socialist Republic of Albania" (Tirana, 1976), p. 167.
4. "Light music", which sometimes features rock-style syncopation or drumming, is perhaps the nearest Albanian equivalent to pop music; it is nevertheless easy to relate to folk music - at times so much so that it is difficult to detect where one stops and the other begins.
5. Spiro Kalemi: "Arritjet e artit tonë muzikor" (Achievements of our Musical Art); Tirana; 1982; p. 152.
6. Simon Gjoni: "The Modernist Distortions in Contemporary Bourgeois-Revisionist Music", in: "Albania Today"; 1977, No. 1; p. 48-52.

MUZIKA NË SHQIPËRI
nga Dave Smith

Për sa i përket muzikës në Shqipëri, pasuria dhe larmia e saj të habit, po të merret parasysh fakti se vendi ka një popullësi rreth tre milionë banorë, që popullojnë një hapësirë pak ma të madhe (madje edhe më malore) se krahina e Uellsit. Me sa duket, kënga është sport kombëtar më popullor sesa futbolli. Jo aq e çuditshme, meqë edhe pas një vizite në një kopsht fëmijësh, pashë se të vegjëlit janë në gjendje të këndojnë e recitojnë vjersha me vetëbesim të jashtëzakonshëm, zotësi e ndërgjegje. Grupet muzikore prej tri deri në pesë instrumentesh luajnë nëpër bare, restaurante e hotele dhe shpesh përfshijnë një instrumentist virtuoz, një klarinetist ose një violinist: shkathtësia teknike, cilësia e tonit të plotë, lulesat e komplikuara, dhe glissandet e shpeshta kontribuojnë në natyrën rapsodike gazmore të performancave së tyre.

Këto lloj orkestrinash, të njohura si *saze*, përfshijnë edhe instrumente të tilla si piano, kitarë (herë-herë elektrike) dhe daulle, dhe janë tipike për muzikën popullore urbane, format e të cilit u zhvilluan përgjatë pushtimit 500 vjeçar turk. Pavarësisht disa veçorive orientale, ajo tingëllon tepër shqiptare (më tepër se muzika e Ballkanit) sepsa ka një bazë folkloristike veçanërisht të ndryshme.

Edhe midis krahinave të ndryshme ka larmi, e sidomos muzika vokale e cila priret kah muzika homofonike në Veri dhe polifonisë komplekse, me tingëllim të lashtë polifonik në Jug, ku mënyrat se si duhet të këndojë çdo pjesëtar grupi janë zhvilluar më tepër se në çdo rajon të Evropës. Ansamblet floklorike instrumentale shpeshherë përdorin lahutë me qafë të gjatë dhe fyejt e barinjve. Ndonëse lahutat zakonisht shoqërojnë këngët, instrumentet si fyjet (*fyelli* dhe *kavalli*) si dhe klarineta e vogël dyshe (*zumarja*) nganjëherë dëgjohen më mirë kur luhen vetëm;[1] zakonisht duke përdorur frymëmarrje rrethore, në këto instrumente solistët improvizojnë "pjesë" duke u bazuar në përsëritje të shpeshta dhe të larmishme të motiveve të thjeshta. Një ekuivalent në muzikën urbane (dhe një nga pjesët e saj kryesore) është *kaba*,

> ...improvizim instrumental i një shtrirjeje të madhe territoriale;
> ...siç ndodh me Blues në SHBA, dhimbja nga tingujt e kabës është familjare, por gjithmonë e ndryshme dhe e njomë.[2]

Grupet muzikore që këndojnë për turistët, shpesh bëjnë muzikë dhe luajnë edhe ndonjë melodi perëndimore, të cilat i plotësojnë me shprehje e zbukurime shqiptare; dhe me sa duket kanë njëfarë prirjeje për tango dhe këngë popullore të njohura — "Petite Fleur" dhe "House of the Rising Sun" janë më të dashurat e tyre.

Muzika popullore shqiptare, pra, është një forcë kulturore tejet aktive. Arkivi i muzikës floklorike i Institutit të Kulturës Popullore në Tiranë përmban rreth 21.000 melodi popullore. "Ky mund të duket si koleksion i gjerë" më tha nëndrejtori i institutit, "por s'është asgjë në krahasim me atë që duhet të kishim". Janë të shpeshta konkurset dhe festivalet kombëtare dhe rajonale, ndër të cilat më i njohuri është Festivali Kombëtar i Folklorit, që mbahet në Gjirokastër, një qytet piktoresk, i njohur për arkitekturën e tij unike. Ky festival mbahet çdo pesë vjet, më së fundi u mbajt në tetor, 1978.

Falë punës së madhe të të ndjerit A. L. Lloyd, muzika folklorike shqiptare nuk është krejt e panjohur në Britani. Po çfarë krijojnë kompozitorët shqiptarë? Shfaqja e John Jansson-it që dha Tokatën e Çesk Zade-së para simpatizantëve të Shqipërisë në takimin përkujtimor për A. L. Lloyd-in në janar, ishte mbase shfaqja e parë britanike e një kompozimi shqiptar. Por sado pak të njohur të jenë këta kompozitorë për pjesën tjetër të botës, ata janë të njohur e çmohen shumë përbrenda vendit të tyre.

Duke qenë i pajisur me një radio-kasetë e një gazetë të përditshme, unë arrita të regjistroj mjaft muzikë orkestrale, korale dhe operistike. Prej një udhërrëfyesi u informova se kompozitorët shqiptarë bazohen në folklorin e vendit dhe shmangin

> ...prirjet abstrakte dhe dekadente. Synimi i tyre estetik është "kombëtar në formë dhe socialist në substance", parim bazë i realizmit socialist.[3]

Prisja të dëgjoja më shumë muzikë që varej nga kompozitorët nacionalistë të shekullit të 19 dhe fillim-shekullit të 20 dhe kompozitorët realistë socialistë sovjetikë të epokës së Stalinit. Këto pritshmëri ushqeheshin nga njohuria se kushtet e krijuara nga pushtimi turk, rrënimet e pas luftës si dhe diktatura represive e mes dy luftërave e mbretit Zog e kishin bërë të pamundur përparimin e kompozitorëve. Praktikisht, menjëherë pas viteve të pasluftës, kompozitorëve ju desht të fillonin prej kurrëgjësë. Rrjedhimisht, opereta e parë shqiptare, "Agimi" nga Kristo Kono, u dha në vitin 1953, opera e parë "Mrika" e Prenk Jakovës në vitin 1958 ndërkaq baleti i parë "Halili dhe Hajrija" i Tish Daisë, me 1963.

Përshtypjet e mia të para për shumë nga ato që dëgjoja ishin të përziera. Shumica e pjesëve ishin tërheqëse e të këndshme, plot vrull dhe gazmore, dhe të gjitha ishin tonale (në kuptimin më të gjerë të fjalës). Por shpesh, më linin të hutuar nga një qëndrim i çuditshëm që kishin ndaj progresionit harmonik, ose shkallës së ndryshimit të ideve shumë më të shpejtë sesa, po themi, "Rapsodia për piano dhe orkestër" e Sokol Shupos — një shembull veçanërisht i pakuptueshëm. Mbase, më çorientues ishte fakti se shpesh herë ishte e vështirë t'i ndërlidhje këto vepra me modelet perëndimore. Kisha dëgjuar vetëm një pjesë — "Pjesë për malësorët" e Lorenc Antonit — që mund të akuzohej për një mbetjeborxh të fortë (ndaj Dvořák); frymat e pritshme të Bartók-ut dhe Prokofiev-it ishin të rralla, megjithëse nganjëherë vihej re një gamë orkestrale me tinguj të turbullt rus. Radio-Tirana, transmetonte shpesh programe me rapsodi, poema simfonike, suita, muzikë baleti si dhe uvertura. Një kompozitor, muzika e të cilit transmetohej shpesh dhe që më tërhoqi vëmendjen ishte Aleksandër

Peçi (i lindur me 1951). Rapsodia e tij për violinë dhe orkestër (1977) ishte tipike. E titulluar "Vallja jonë — valle e popullit" ajo pasqyron kontaktin e kompozitorit me muzikën popullore të jugut, veçanërisht asaj të Përmetit, një qytet afër kufirit grek, muzika e të cilit shquhet për ngrohtësinë lirike dhe karakterin e gjallë. Kjo vepër është një shembull i mirë që vë në kontrast këto dy lloj materialesh — që prezanton një melodi autentike popullore lirike, para se ta nisë drejt një kadence të shkurtër e mahnitëse që shpërfaq llojshmërinë e kabasë. Poashtu kjo vepër dëshmon për lidhjen me folklorin pa e kthyer atë në një aranzhim të sofistikuar. Qartësia dhe tërheqja e menjëhershme duket edhe në veprat e tjera të Peçit për instrument soli dhe orkestër, veçanërisht "Fantazia për violonçel" (1979). "Variacionet për korno" (1975) është një pjesë tjetër e tij (nuk kisha dëgjuar kurrë një instrumentist në korno të përdorte aq shumë vibrato), por suita për piano dhe orkestër e titulluar "Kuadro heroizmi" është më disonante dhe më e ngarkuar dhe poashtu përmban lulesa që ta kujtojnë Prokofiev-in. "Pjesë për flaut", e shoqëruar nga orkestra folklorike thuajse latino-amerikane, ka karakter "të lehtë" dhe pasqyron faktin se Peçi, si shumica e kompozitorëve të tjerë shqiptarë, është i qetë kur shkruan muzikë filmi, po aq sa është kur shkruan ndonjë këngë emocionuese revolucionare.[4]

Jo të gjithë kompozitorët arrijnë t'i referohen kaq qartë muzikës popullore si Peçi. Disa kompozitorë duket të jenë të pasionuar pas tensioneve të tonaliteteve minore. Një pjesë ku përdoren teknika të tilla është Rapsodia nr. 1 për orkestër (1973) e Feim Ibrahimit (i lindur me 1937). Në një libër mbi kompozitorët shqiptarë kisha lexuar se kjo pjesë

> ... ngjall direkt rapsoditë autentike folklorike[5]

E admirova veprën për dramën e saj emocionale dhe forcën, por nuk arrita të shquaja ndonjë lidhje shumë të fortë folklorike. Besoj se shumica e dëgjuesve perëndimorë do t'i pëlqenin poemat simfonike "Atdheu" (1974) të Shpëtim Kushtës (l. 1946) dhe "Borova" të Thoma Gaqit (l. 1948) pa qenë në dijeni se kanë ndonjë referim folklorik. Solemniteti dhe epizmi e përshkojnë të parën, ndërsa "Borova" — që e ka marrë titullin nga një fshat, banorët e të cilit u masakruan prej nazistëve — është e mbushur me tragjedi dhe pasqyron guximin e popullit i cili luftoi kundër pushtuesve. Orkestrimi i këtyre poemave simfonike është kryesisht i errët e me ngjyra të forta, një tipar që ndeshet vazhdimisht në muzikën shqiptare. Muzika e Peçit ka teksturë më transparente, por ajo e Tish Daisë ka një tingullim më individual. Rapsodia e Daisë për flaut dhe orkestër (1981) është pjesë e shkurtër, por tërheqëse e shkruar me teknikë të lartë ornamentimi, lirike pastorale e em regjistër të ulët flauti, që lidhet më shpejt e me pasion më të pastër me orkestrën. Shkrimi i vargut është veçanërisht imagjinativ, duke filluar nga figurat e arpezhit të mprehta (që ta kujtojnë Janaček) në tuttis deri tek shoqërimi i qetë. Shkrimi efektiv me vargje është gjithashtu një veçori e një fragmenti që pata dëgjuar nga një vepër shumë më e hershme "Halili dhe Hajrija" (1961-2). Ngjarjet e portretizuara në këtë balet të parë shqiptar, vendosen në shekullin e 18, kur pushtimi turk hasi në rezistencën e malësorëve shqiptarë. Muzikalisht, pjesa tregon aftësisë së

Daisë për të vepruar me kontraste pa ta krijuar atë ndjenjën se kompozitori po jep shumë informacion – në fakt, idetë e Daisë duket se kanë një ritëm më të qetë se sa ato të shumicës së kolegëve të tij.

Mes viteve 1963 dhe 1973, "Halili dhe Hajrija" ishte performuar rreth 150 herë, që në njëfarë pike edhe e tregon popullaritetin e saj. Të inkurajuar nga suksesi i kësaj pjese, në vitet '60 u shfaqën edhe disa balete të tjera si "Delina" e Çesk Zadesë), "Fatosi Partizan" nga Kozma Laro, dhe "Cuca e Maleve" e Nikolla Zoraqit. Tabloja e dytë e aktit të dytë e baletit të Zoraqit, (një nga gjërat më mbresëlënëse që pata dëgjuar gjatë qëndrimit tim) dëshmon se kompozitori ka prirje të theksuara lirike dhe nota të forta pasionale. "Uvertura festive" (1969) mezi njihet si vepra e të njëjtit kompozitor meqë është jashtëzakonisht festive dhe e gëzueshme. Arrita ta blej edhe veprën për piano të "Koncertit të tretë për violinë" të Zoraqit, e cila është djallëzisht e vështirë si vepër, por duke gjykuar nga interpretimi joshës i Ibrahim Malit nga performanca e Rapsodisë së Peçit, ekzistojnë disa violinistë që janë të aftë për ta performuar dhe për t'i dalë në krye.

Njëri ndër profilet më të njohur është edhe kompozitori Tonin Harapi (l. 1928), vepra e të cilit duket mjaft diatonike në krahasim me atë të shumicës së kolegëve të tij. Suita e tij vokale "Vullnetarët" (1965) i kushtohet rinisë së vendit, puna vullnetare e të cilës është mirë e njohur në ndërtimin e hekurudhave; një pjesë korale gazmore dhe energjike me tre kohë, e cila e nderon këtë fenomen të sotëm. Harapi duket të jetë më pak i tërhequr nga lloji i shprehjes së pasionuar që është e zakonshme për veprat e Ibrahimit, Zoraqit dhe Kushtës, madje edhe në veprat dramatike të tij si opera "Zgjimi" (1974). Vepra e tij "Rapsodia e dytë për piano dhe orkestër" (vepër që aludon dukshëm në muzikën folklorike) duket se e vërteton këtë.

Do të kisha dashur të dëgjoja më shumë për arritjet operistike të kompozitorëve të vjetër të Shqipërisë si Prenk Jakova (1919 - 69) dhe Kristo Kono (l. 1907), të dytë artistë të akredituar të popullit (mes të tjerëtve: Tish Daia, Çesk Zadeja dhe Avni Mula, ndërsa disa të tjerë Artistë të Meritës). Opera e Konos "Lulja e kujtimit" (1958) kulminon me një finale marciale mahnitëse dhe tingëllon si një bashkëpunimi midis Verdit dhe Eisler.

Muzika shqiptare zë një vend të veçantë në botën e kompozimit. Është një muzikë që elementin e komunikimit e ka të rëndësisë së veçantë dhe të parë. Realisht, edhe pse disa prej kompozimeve që dëgjova më erdhën si të rëndomta e të pamenduara mirë, shumica e tyre më dhanë freski. Për këto 40 vjet, kompozitorët e Shqipërisë kanë krijuar e përparuar ndonëse muzika e tyre i injoron prirjet e muzikës perëndimore. Arsyet e tyre për këtë fenomen qëndrojnë në një qëndrim politik popullor, i cili pohon se

> ...përpjekjet e estetëve reaksionarë të sotëm për të reklamuar një art 'universal' i shërbejnë interesit të borgjezisë imperialiste, e cila gjithmonë është përpjekur të denigrojë ose eliminojë traditat kulturore të kombeve më të vogla dhe frymën kombëtare në art dhe kulturë, për ta lehtësuar agresionin e saj kulturor dhe nënshtrimin e kombeve... duke filluar nga impresionizmi dhe ekspresionizmi

(dhe duke vazhduar) e deri te muzika e sotme dodekafonike, dhe e përpiktë... të gjithë përpiqen të justifikohen nën petkun e 'risisë', 'kërkimin e të resë me çdo kusht, duke prishur çdo lidhje me traditat përparimtare të popujve dhe, mbi të gjitha, duke kërkuar të largojë vëmendjen nga problemet thelbësore të përmbajtjes, nga çështjet kryesore që shqetësojnë njerëzimin sot, klasën punëtore, rininë, popujt e botës që po luftojnë për çlirimin dhe të drejtat e tyre sociale.[6]

SHËNIMET

1. Pllaka që përmban solo të instrumenteve të ndryshme është "Folklore instrumental albanais" (Vendemiaire VDE 114, AD 37). Dy pllakat e tjera të cilat mund t'i rekomandoj janë: "L'Albanie folklorique" (Disques Cellier 010) dhe "Folk Music of Albania", të mbledhura dhe të ripërpunuara nga A. L. Lloyd (Topic 12T 154).
2. A. L. Lloyd: Shënime mbi kapakun mbështjellës të "Folk Music of Albania".
3. "Përmbledhje e Republikës Popullore Socialiste të Shqipërisë" (Tiranë, 1976), f. 167.
4. "Muzika e lehtë", e cila ndonjëherë përmban sinkopim të stilit rock ose të daulles, është ndoshta ekuivalenti më i afërt shqiptar me muzikën pop; e megjithatë është e lehtë të ndërlidhet me muzikën folklorike – nganjëherë aq shumë, sa bëhet e e vështirë ta dallosh se ku ndalet njëra e ku fillon tjetra.
5. Spiro Kalemi: "Arritjet e artit tonë muzikor"; Tirana; 1982; p. 152.
6. Simon Gjoni: "The Modernist Distortions in Contemporary Bourgeois-Revisionist Music", in: "Albania Today"; 1977, No. 1; p. 48-52.

THE INSTITUTE OF PEOPLE'S CULTURE
by Dave Smith

(This article is fundamentally a report of two meetings with workers from the Institute of People's Culture in Tirana. The first of these meetings took place in August 1981, when I visited the Institute and met the assistant director Mustafa Gërcaliu Tish Daija, one of Albania's leading composers; and Ferial Daja, a young female ethno-musicologist).

The Institute is divided into four sections, of which two are concerned with ethnography and two with folklore. One of the ethnographical sections deals with material culture, which includes the many varied and beautiful national costumes, silk embroideries, carpets and rugs, and the characteristic dwelling-houses notable for their architecture and rooms full of ornamentation and carved woodwork. Another section concentrates on social and spiritual culture — investigating the ways of life, such as weddings, movement of the population, death and other demographic concerns. The ethnographic archive contains some 25,000 items ranging from carpets and national costumes to pottery and agricultural tools. The other two sections make up what was originally the Institute of Folklore, which was founded in 1960. The literary section covers folk prose and poetry (and includes tales, proverbs, riddles and anecdotes) of many different genres — epic, legendary, historical and folk-lyrical, for example. About forty books have already been published by this section and the archive contains about a million verses. A collection of some 15,000 proverbs is in preparation.

The musical and choreographic section deals with the highly varied folk music and dances and the development of folklore. I was shown the archive which includes nearly 21,000 recordings of folk music, systemized and catalogued for easy reference, films of 600 dances, another 200 films concerning costumes and weddings, as well as catalogues of folk melodies and folk lyrics. This seemed an enormous collection for a small country, but Mustafa Gërcaliu indicated that they considered it "small in comparison to what we <u>must</u> have". An extensive historical study of folk instruments will be published shortly, as well as a two-volume work on folk dances arranged according to geographical location and content.

The work of the Institute is, like the economy of the country, planned in advance. The collection and study of different cultural phenomena and the publication of the results of such studies constitute major concerns. During the present five-year plan (1981-85) they intend to produce 45 books. Extensive areas of work are not carried out by just a single individual — for instance, Ferial Daja was part of a group working on a project which involved detailed analysis of the best songs heard at three national folk festivals which took place at Gjirokastra in 1968, 1973 and 1978. Furthermore, it would be difficult for the 60 employees of the Institute to carry out their activities without the assistance of volunteers and associate workers from all walks of life spread throughout the country. They collect materials, participate in scientific discussions and give opinions about publications.

Students at the Higher Institute of Arts also participate in investigative expeditions — indeed, it is an essential part of their practice, since folklore is not just a peripheral part of the studies of musicians and dancers. For instance, in the School of Choreography folk dances are taught as well as the classical repertoire and Albanian ballets display elements of both. Choreographers and composers often come to the Institute to study — Tish Daia works there and therefore has a foot in both camps, but he was quick to point out that all Albanian composers study folklore in order that their work may have a truly Albanian national foundation. Instrumentalists learn folk instruments in school and folklore constitutes an element within the normal middle school curriculum. Any visitor can hear the influence of folk music in the bands that play in the tourist hotels even when they are playing Western tunes.

In August 1983, I had an equally interesting (and good-humored) encounter with folk dance specialist Skënder Selimi and ethnomusicologist Beni Kruta. I was particularly pleased to meet Kruta since A. L. Lloyd had once indicated in a letter that he considered him to be

> ...a brilliant musicologist, particularly in respect of musical folklore. He has it in him to become a world figure in that field.

The Institute's archive was progressing well — for instance, some 4,000 recordings of folk music and 400 films of folk dances had been added since 1981. The Institute's main preoccupation at that time was the National Folk Festival at Gjirokastra (held every five years) which took place from the 6th. to 12th. October 1983. This constituted the grand finale of an event of mass participation — the preliminary stages, which took place last year, involved some 2,300 groups and 69,000 people. This festival begins in the brigades of the co-operatives or the departments of the factories and then proceeds in an unbroken chain at the level of the village, zone, town and district — the most distinguished representatives going forward to the national festival.

A committee of specialists chooses those songs, dances and instrumental pieces which are considered to be of the greatest scientific value and, although this involves judgment of both the old and the new, the festival does not admit altered or modernized folk music (there is another festival for this category). The principal aim is the presentation and preservation of traditional techniques and the varied characteristics of different parts of the country. At Gjirokastra, each of the 26 districts presents a programme of 30 to 45 minutes duration — essentially a selection of what is available but one which is utterly typical of that district. The festival is filmed and relayed to the population by means of radio and television.

Beni Kruta also spoke of an important symposium that will have taken place immediately before the festival itself. Entitled "The Legendary Heroic Epic", this symposium focused on a literary musical form found in Northern Albania and adjacent areas of Yugoslavia and is most familiar to folk music enthusiasts as a semi-improvised vocal performance of sometimes several hours duration with the accompaniment of the *lahuta* (in Yugoslavia, the *gusle*), a one-stringed fiddle. The symposium presented an all-round scientific analysis, examining many aspects of the genre — musicological, literary, ethnographic, historical, linguistic, folklorist, etc.

Foreign specialists have always considered this to be an essentially Slavic creation dating from the late Middle Ages. Most of these scholars have been ignorant of the Albanian contribution, and a lack of publication on the Albanian side did not help. But since Liberation the Institute has published a good deal about the Northern heroic epic. Taken together with materials published before Liberation, Albanians have come to the conclusion that this form of culture originated in Albania rather than having been inherited from the Slavs. This is not to say that the genre is uninfluenced or separate from the culture of neighboring countries. But the Balkan origins are thought to predate the 7th. century when the Slavs entered the area.

Beni Kruta also indicated that the musical aspects have largely been ignored — to separate the very long texts from the music was, he felt, a basic error of scholarship, since the two were always connected. He also stated that, contrary to what many Western publications maintain, the readily apparent differences in vocal practice between North and South are mirrored in the instrumental folk music. In addition, certain instruments found in the North are not used in the South (and vice versa). For an instrument such as the *fyell* (a shepherd's pipe) the Southern repertoire is rhythmically freer and the music more descriptive and panoramic than in the North.

Folk dances, too, display these very characteristics — solo dances dominating in the North and group dances in the South. Skënder Selimi pointed out an interesting development within dance whereby old ritual elements of patriarchal times are being replaced by elements more in tune with the new socialist consciousness, a phenomenon unique to Albania. These new elements have made their strongest impact on humorous and wedding dances. Also the development of group dancing is encouraged (especially in the North) as well as dances accompanied by singing.

In 1981, Mustafa Gërcaliu pointed out that the Gjirokastra Folk Festival serves as a fine example to counter views which allege that folklore has lost its role in the century of technical progress, that its use is only for commercial purposes or tourism, that now it is destined to be locked up in archives and museums and is useful only to historians. He criticized the kind of Western propaganda which promotes the cosmopolitanising of culture and art and which claims that the stage of national schools has passed. Albania maintains that this is aimed at opening the way for ideological diversion in order to destroy the culture of the peoples. Hence the struggle to preserve national features in art and to develop and enrich popular culture becomes even more important today.

— *Albanian Life*, no 27, 1983

ALBANIAN COMPOSERS — UNIQUE IN EUROPE
A View From an English Composer

Q — How have you managed to become familiar with the music of Albanian composers?

DAVE SMITH Whenever I've visited Albania as a tourist, I've made a point of recording as much as possible from Radio Tirana and buying scores from shops. A book by Spiro Kalemi [Arritjet e artit tonë muzikor — 1982] was a great help and more recently Albanian musicians have given me photocopies of unpublished pieces. So now I possess about 100 cassettes of both folk and composed music as well as a good number of scores.

Q — And why do you say that Albanian composers occupy a unique position in European musical culture?

DAVE — For a number of reasons. Albania is the only European country which had virtually no artistic musical culture before forty-five years ago. Since then the state has encouraged the development of its musical tradition and created orchestras, ensembles and educational institutions. Also, it's very generous in its support of composers, and they genuinely want to reach a wide audience. To a greater or lesser extent their work relates to folk music which is quite natural in the circumstances and certainly not anachronistic). They do this without trying to mix in elements of avant-garde styles as some contemporary Romanian composers do. Many adapt their style depending on the task at hand, whether it be concert music, opera, film music, a revolutionary song or light music: it doesn't seem very usual to specialise. In Britain, of course, this kind of adaptability is not common, Albanian musical tradition, being young, is developing at quite a fast rate. First of all, you had the extraordinary position of a composer like Kristo Kono — a 20th Century composer without a heritage. There are half a dozen or so composers born between 1926 and 1931 who built on these beginnings and who, as far as I know, are all still active. These include Tish Daija — he produced the first ballet in 1963 and the first-string quartet ten years earlier: Çesk Zadeja, also composed the first symphony in 1956: Pjetër Gaci who wrote the first concerto — for violin — in 1959. When you get to composers born about twenty years later like Thoma Gaqi and Aleksandër Peçi advances in sophistication and technique have accelerated the groundwork had been done by the time they started writing. And younger composers such as Thoma Simaku and David Tukiqi are demonstrating that they want to continue these advances rather than to feed off the successes of ten years before. Of course, the older composers have advanced too, so it's much easier for an Albanian composer of any age to write a symphony in 1990 than it was in 1960. It's going to sound very different as well. And this leads to another point which is that socialist realism has always been scorned in the West as producing works which are mediocre, simplistic, unimaginative and lacking in individuality. If you compare and assess a few good works by composers like Feim Ibrahimi, Tonin Harapi, Thoma Gaqi and Limoz Dizdari. I think it would be pretty easy to demolish this view.

Q — You sound very enthusiastic about these composers. Aren't you in danger of over-estimating their worth simply because you're well disposed towards the country as well as appreciating their disadvantaged position?

DAVE No, I don't think so. When I was at university I asked one of my tutors what abilities he considered a music student should possess by the time he or she had graduated. Amongst other things, he replied, "the ability to differentiate the good works of Bach, Mozart and Beethoven from the bad ones". As far as Albanian music is concerned, I obviously have preferences and some pieces, some composers even, don't impress me at all. But I think there's a surprising amount of good work given the size and population of the country and its brief artistic musical history. And it deserves a wider audience — after all, it's not heard much outside Albania.

For example, I think there are several pieces which would be of interest to music students in Western countries. A violinist friend once pointed out that Pjetër Gaci's violin concerto would be an ideal conservatoire piece not only because of its suitable level of difficulty but also because of the stylistic range. There's a decidedly "classical" 1st movement, a very "jolly" 3rd movement and in between a Romance which combines the two elements. Also there's a student of mine who told me recently that Thoma Gaqi's cello concerto is the first cello piece she's felt genuinely enthusiastic about learning.

Q What was it that made her say that?

DAVE She's attracted by the energetic, almost berserk nature of the music, and also the frequent and effective double-stopping. The way he constantly develops his material is engaging as is his fondness for unpredictable bar-lengths.

You can find some of. the same qualities in the Rhapsody "Shqipëria në festë" and the symphonic dances and more especially in the Poem-concerto and Ballade, both for violin and orchestra. The solo opening of the Ballade is so powerful that I almost regret the first orchestra 1 entry.

Q So what area of music do you find most interesting? Opera? Piano music? Orchestral music?

DAVE I've never been much interested in opera so I've been intentionally lazy as far as Albanian opera is concerned. I'm very interested in piano music generally but I don't know much by Albanian composers. Much of what I have heard sounds rather unadventurous and unidiomatically written for the instrument, although I'd certainly have to exclude some of the larger pieces of Kozma Lara (the ballads and sonatas, for instance) from that criticism. I've found that many of my favourite Albanian pieces are for orchestra with solo instrument, especially violin.

Q Is there any particular reason for this, or do you just like the violin?

DAVE Almost every composer I've come across seems to have written at least one work for violin. Amongst those I've heard, whether I like them or not, I can't think of any which are ill-conceived in terms of the instrument. Possibly one reason for this is because there's a strong connection between the way the violin is used as a folk instrument and the kind of bravura writing you find in the works of the European late Romantics and after. And there are a lot of good violinists in Albania which is encouraging if you're a composer. I mentioned the Gaqi works earlier, but there are many others I'd recommend — Peçi's 2nd Rhapsody (Vallja jonë, valle e popullit), Ibrahimi's Rhapsody, Tish Daija's Poem, Shaçir Kodra's Poem, Dizdari's Lirikë fshatare, Zadeja's Rhapsody, Lejla Agolli's Rondo, Simaku's Ballade and Scherzo and probably a lot more besides.

Q	How about pieces for clarinet? That's a popular folk instrument.
DAVE	Yes, but the way composers of whatever nationality have written for the clarinet is light-years away from the way in which Albanian folk musicians play. But I haven't encountered any particularly memorable clarinet works apart from Ethem Qerimi's Kaba. I presume he falls into the category of the folk musician who composes — I know he plays kabas on the violin — so he's probably a special case.
Q	What about other instruments like piano or flute?
DAVE	As far as works for piano and orchestra are concerned, it seems odd that few composers seem willing to write orchestrally for the piano or, at least, to treat the piano as a "big" instrument. The kind of expansive gestures you'd find in the works of related Western composers seem to be avoided by Albanians. Zadeja's concerto is a notable exception, and the opening of Peçi's concerto attempts to out-Prokofiev Prokofiev. Apart from the Zadeja concerto, Kozma Lara's rhapsodies and concertos seem to be the positive achievements in this area. As for flute, the most successful composer is Tish Daija — there's a good Rhapsody, the Valle Devolliçe and a delightfully quixotic Fantasy for four flutes. There doesn't seem to be that much written for other wind instruments although I get the impression that steps are being taken to remedy this in recent years. Ibrahimi's oboe concerto and Tukiqi's bassoon concerto are the first Albanian concertos for these instruments and, as such, they're remarkably successful being both well written and musically convincing. And on the subject of recent developments, double and triple concertos have started to appear as well as works for string orchestra. I suspect that Ibrahim Madhi has been instrumental in encouraging string works — he's one of the, country's leading violinists — at least, his name is associated with many of the performances.
Q	You said earlier that you thought that Albanian music is stylistically varied. Can you enlarge on that a bit?
DAVE	OK, let's take a couple of examples from composers I feel have a particularly individual voice — Tish Daija's flute rhapsody "Bjeshkëve te larta" and Ibrahimi's violin rhapsody "Kënga në Bjeshkë" — I think they both relate to folk music of the same area, but I could be wrong.

Tish Daija's work looks quite simple from the score with its sustained major and minor chords. He has a fondness for clear airy textures, a good example of which appears in the middle section in which the soloist plays against a backdrop of pentatonic chord clusters on strings. The melodic element is a quotation from a folk source — I've heard the original played on kavalls. This contrasts sharply with the passionate orchestral tuttis appearing elsewhere. Harmonically speaking the tension is encouraged most by augmented chords, and although that doesn't sound daring, it's effective, as is his orchestration, I'd say that he is one of the most imaginative orchestrators, together with Nikolla Zoraqi.

On the other hand, Ibrahimi's Rhapsody tends to avoid major and minor chords altogether, displaying (like some of his other works) a preference for perfect intervals (4ths and 5ths) with semitonal dissonances. There's a natural preference for linear writing and counterpoint, in contrast with the predominant homophony of Daija's work, a far darker orchestration and a far greater sense of struggle. So, the works are quite different, but |

	I imagine that both these composers would prefer to stress the points in common between their compositional attitudes rather than their differences in stylistic approach. And both works appear to contain specific, as distinct from generalised, folk characteristics.
Q	To what kind of Western composers would you relate this music?
DAVE	That's not always easy to say — it's a unique musical culture as I've said. The attitude to harmonic progression, for instance, is a bit peculiar if you're not used to it. Even now I find some of Zadeja's work difficult to follow — for this reason, although I have no problem with his piano concerto. But the 19th and 20th century Romantics, particularly of the nationalist school, are relevant as are some Soviet composers.

This may give the impression that the music sounds dated or anachronistic (especially with titles like "Rhapsody"), but I'd contest that view despite their rejection of 20th century modernist trends. Zoraqi's ballet "Cuca e Malëve" employs a technique of thematic transformation obviously derived from Liszt, but it doesn't sound at all like a 19th century work. A deeper familiarity with the work, of Bartok seems only to have occurred recently, but I feel that the works which reflect this development could only have been written with today's view of music and music history. Passion, heroism and lament aren't current fashionable features of much European music, but they're common features of Albanian music, both folk and composed, and this is hardly surprising considering the country's history. |
| Q | You've painted quite a detailed picture of Albanian music... |
| DAVE | Hardly, I've only really talked in detail about a single area of concert music. And there are some worthy composers such as Shpëtim Kushta, Kujtim Laro or Sokol Shupo, who I've not even mentioned. You haven't learnt anything about Zadeja's orchestral music, Ibrahimi's vocal symphonic poems or anything much by Peçi or Harapi. And despite having a reasonable collection, I've heard very few complete major works like concertos, symphonies and ballets so I've probably done a disservice to someone somewhere along the line. There's probably some composer who's written a brilliant concerto for clarinet or piano who's feeling pretty sore right now... |

KOMPOZITORËT SHQIPTARË — UNIKË NË EVROPË
Nga pikëpamja e një kompozitori anglez

P   Si arritët të familjarizoheni me muzikën e kompozitorëve shqiptarë?

DAVE SMITH Sa herë që vizitoja Shqipërinë si turist, i vija vetes detyrë të regjistroja sa kisha mundësi nga muzika që jepte Radio Tirana dhe të blija partitura. Një libër nga Spiro Kalemi ("Arritjet e artit tonë muzikor", 1982) më ndihmoi shumë; po ashtu kohët e fundit, muzikantët shqiptarë më kanë dhuruar fotokopje të partiturave të tyre. Kështu që, tani kam rreth 100 kaseta me muzikë folklorike dhe të kultivuar si edhe një numër të madh partiturash.

P   E pse thoni se kompozitorët shqiptarë zënë një vend të rëndësishëm në kulturën evropiane?

DAVE Për një numër arsyesh. Shqipëria është i vetmi vend evropian që pothuajse nuk ka pasur kulturë të kultivuar muzikore 45vjet më parë. Që atëherë shteti e ka inkurajuar zhvillimin e traditës muzikore dhe ka krijuar orkestra ansamble dhe institucione muzikore. Gjithashtu, ai është shumë bujar në mbështetjen që iu bën kompozitorëve dhe ata me të vërtetë kërkojnë të kenë një publik sa më të gjerë. Në pjesën më të madhe, veprat e tyre mbështeten në muzikën folklorike, gjë që është krejt e natyrshme për rrethanat dhe, sigurisht aspak anakronike. Ata e bëjnë këtë pa u përpjekur të përzjejnë elernentë të stileve avangardiste siç bëjnë disa kompozitorë bashkëkohorë. Shumë e adoptojnë stilin e tyre në vartësi të punës që kanë në dorë, qoftë ke një koncert, një operë, muzikë filmi, një këngë e muzikës së lehtë, nuk ndodhi shpesh që të ketë specializime të ngushta. Në Britani, natyrisht, kjo lloj përshtetje nuk është fort e përhapur. Tradita muzikore shqiptare, duke qenë e re, po zhvillohet rne një ritëm shumë të shpejtë. Fillimisht kemi rastin e jashtëzakonshëm të një kompozitori si Kristo Kono — një kompozitor i shekullit të 20, pa asnjë trashëgimi të mëparshme. Pastaj vijnë rreth 6 kompozitorë, të lindur nga vitet 1926 deri më 1931 të cilët u përpoqën në këto fillime, dhe që, me sa di unë, kanë ende veprimtari sot. Këtu përfshihet Tish Daia — ka krijuar baletin e parë më 1963 dhe të parin kuartet harqesh, — Pjetër Gaci, që shkruajti koncertin e parë (për violinë) në 1959. Kur arrin të kompozitorë të lindur 20 vjet më vonë si Thoma Gaqi dhe Aleksandër Peçi, përparimi në sofistikim dhe teknikë është i dukshëm, — tashmë themelet janë hedhur përpara se ata të fillojnë të shkruajnë. Edhe kompozitorë më të rinj si Thoma Simaku e David Tukiqi po tregojnë se dëshirojnë më tepër ta vazhdojnë këtë përparim se sa të ngopen me sukseset e 10 vjetëve të shkuara. Natyrisht edhe kompozitorët e vjetër kanë avancuar gjithashtu, kështu që është shumë më e lehtë per një kompozitor të çfarëdo moshe të shkruajë një simfoni në vitin 1990 se sa ishte në 1960. Gjithashtu ajo do të tingëllojë më ndryshe. Dhe kjo të nxjerr në një pikë tjetër, që realizmi socialist gjithmonë ishte përbuzur në Perëndim se prodhon vepra mediokre, të thjeshtëzuara, pa imagjinatë, dhe me mungesë individualiteti. Po të dëgjoni dhe të krahasoni vetëm disa pjesë të mira nga Feim Ibrahimi, Tonin Harapi, Thoma Gaqi e Limoz Disdari, jam i sigurt se do ta kini të lehtë ta hidhni poshtë këtë pikpamje.

P   Na dukeni shumë entuziast për këta kompozitorë. A mos jeni në rrezik, t'i mbivlerësoni këta, thjesht sepse jeni i predispozuar për mirë ndaj vendit të tyre?

DAVE	Jo. Nuk besoj. Kur isha në Universitet pyeta një nga profesorët e mi se çfarë aftësish duhet të kishte një student muzike në kohën kur diplomohej. Midis të tjerash ai mu përgjigj: aftësinë të diferencojë veprat e mira të Bahut, Moxartit e Bethovenit, nga të këqiat. Përsa i përket muzikës shqiptare, është e qartë që unë kam parapëlqimet e mia, ndërsa disa vepra, madje disa kompozitorë, nuk më bëjnë asnjë përshtypje. Por mendoj se ka çuditërisht shumë vepra dhe shumë kompozitorë të mirë, po të kemi parasysh për masat e vendit, numrin e popullsisë dhe historinë e shkurtër të muzikës së kultivuar. Dhe ajo meriton një audiencë më të gjerë, sepse, në fund të fundit, nuk është shumë e përhapur përtej kufijve të Shqipërisë. Për shembull, mendoj se ka disa pjesë të cilat do të ishin me interes për mjaft studentë në vendet perëndimore. Një miku im violinist, më vuri një ditë në dukje se koncerti për violinë i Pjetër Gacit do të ishte një pjesë ideale për t'u studiuar, jo vetëm për shkallën e tij të përshtatshme të vështirësisë, por gjithashtu edhe për veçoritë stilistike. Ka një kohë të parë thellësisht "klasike", një kohë të tretë shumë folklorike dhe, midis tyre, një Romancë, që i kombinon të dy elementet. Gjithashtu një studente më tha para disa kohësh se koncerti për violonçel i Thoma Gaqit është e para pjesë për violonçel që i ka ngjallur entuziazmin për ta mësuar.
P	Çfarë e shtyn atë ta thotë një gjë të tillë?
DAVE	Atë e tërheq karakteri energjik, cilësia e lartë e muzikës si dhe dublë kordat e vazhdueshme me plot efekt. Mënyra se si ai e shtjellon vazhdimisht materialin është tërheqëse. Mund t'i gjeni këto cilësi në rapsodinë "Shqipëria në festë" dhe në vallet simfonike e, sidomos, në Poemën Koncert dhe në Balladën, të dyja për violinë dhe orkestër.
P	Atëherë, ç'pjesë të muzikës konsideroni më interesante? Operën? Muzikën pianistike? Muzikën orkestrale?
DAVE	Skam qenë kurrë shumë i interesuar për operën, ndaj me qëllim e kam neglizhuar operën shqiptare. Përgjithësisht jam më tepër i interesuar për muzikë pianistike, ndonëse s'kam dëgjuar shumë nga kompozitorët shqiptarë. Shumica e atyre që kam dëgjuar tingëllojnë paksa të ngurta dhe artificiale, ndonëse do të më duhet që të përjashtoj patjetër Kozma Larën (baladat dhe sonatat e tij p.sh.) nga kjo vërejtje. Kam vënë re se shumë nga pjesët e mia të parapëlqyera janë për orkestër me instrument solo, veçanërisht violinë.
P	Ka ndonjë arsye të veçantë për këtë apo ndodh thjesht ngaqë juve iu pëlqen violina?
DAVE	Gati çdo kompozitor me të cilin jam njohur duhet të ketë shkruar të paktën një vepër për violinë. Ndërmjet atyre që kam dëgjuar, pavarësisht nëse më pëlqejnë ose jo, nuk mund të them për asnjërën që është e keqpërshtatur, përsa i përket instrumentit. Ndoshta një arsye për këtë është sepse ka një lidhje të fortë mes mënyrës se si violina përdoret si një instrument folklorik dhe llojit të të shkruarit harmonik që mund të gjeni në veprat e romantikëve të vonë evropianë e më tej. Gjithashtu ka mjaft violinistë të mirë në Shqipëri, gjë që është inkurajuese për çdo kompozitor. Unë përmenda më lart veprat e Gaqit, por ka edhe shumë të tjerë që mund të rekomandoj — Rapsodia e 2-të e Pecit, Poema e Tish Daisë, Poema e Shaqir Kodrës, "Lirikë fshatare" e Dizdarit, Rapsodia e Zadesë, Rondoja e Lejla Agollit, Balada dhe Skerco e Thoma Simakut e ndoshta, edhe shumë të tjera.
P	Po përsa i përket pjesëve për klarinetë? Ky është një instrument folklorik mjaft popullor.

DAVE   Po, por mënyrën se si kompozitorët e kombësive të ndryshme kanë shkruar për klarinetë, është tepër larg mënyrës se si luajnë instrumentistët popullorë shqiptarë. Unë nuk kam hasur ndonjë pjesë për klarinetë veçanërisht të spikatur, me përjashtim të Kabasë së Ethem Qerimit. Them se ai duhet t'i përkasë kategorisë së instrumentistëve popullorë që edhe kompozojnë, — e di që luan kaba me violinë — ndaj ndoshta ai përbën një rast të veçantë.

P   Po përsa i përket instrumentëve të tjerë si piano apo flauti?

DAVE   Përsa i përket pjesëve për piano dhe orkestër duket e çuditshme që pak kompozitorë dëshirojnë të shkruajnë në mënyrë orkestrale për piano, ose, të paktën ta trajtojnë pianon si një instrument të madh. Veçohet këtu koncerti i Zadesë. Rapsodia dhe koncerti i Kozma Larës, që janë arritje të shquara

Përsa i përket flautit, kompozitori më i suksesshëm është Tish Daija — ka një Rapsodi të mirë, Vallen Devollitçe dhe një fantazi mjaft të këndshme donkishoteske për katër flaute. Nuk duket të jetë shkruar shumë edhe për instrumente të tjerë të frymës, ndonëse kam përshtypjen se ka përpjekje për të përmirësuar gjendjen së shpejti. Koncerti për oboe i Ibrahimit dhe koncerti i Tukiqit për fagot, janë të parët koncerte shqiptarë për këtë instrument dhe, si të tilla, ato janë posaçërisht të suksesshme, duke qenë njëkohësisht të shkruara mirë dhe, veçanërisht, bindëse. Dhe sa për zhvillimet e kohëve të fundit, kanë filluar të dalin koncerte duetesh dhe triosh si edhe vepra për orkestra harqesh. Mendoj se Ibrahim Madhi ka qenë një faktor për interpretimin e veprave për harqe (është një nga violinistët më të mirë të vendit) — të paktën emri i tij lidhet me shumë prej ekzekutimeve.

P   Më parë thatë se mendoni që muzika shqiptare kishte mjaft variacione stilistike. A mund të zgjeroheni pak në këtë pikë?

DAVE   Mirë. Le të marrim nja dy shembuj nga kompozitorë të cilët mendoj se kanë një individualitet të theksuar: Rapsodia për flaut e Tish Daisë "Bjeshkëve të larta" dhe Rapsodia "Këngë në bjeshkë" e Ibrahimit. Mendoj se që të dyja kanë lidhje me muzikën folklorike të të njëjtës krahinë, por ndoshta mund edhe të kem gabuar. Vepra e Tish Daisë duket fare e thjeshtë në partiturë, me ato akorde maxhore e minore të përmbajtura. Ai ka prirje për tekste të qarta, plot ajër e, një shembull i mirë për këtë, duket në pjesën e mesit, në të cilën një solist luan përballë akordeve pentatonike të harqeve. Elementi melodik është citim nga një burim popullor, e kam dëgjuar origjinalin të luajtur me kavall. Kjo kontraston tepër me partin pasionant orkestral, që ndeshet gjetkë. Në planin harmonik tensioni inkurajohet së tepërmi nga zgjerimi i akordeve dhe ndonëse kjo s'tingëllon shumë e guximshme, është e efektshme, siç është edhe orkestrimi. Do të thosha se eshtë një nga orkestruesit më në imagjinatë, së bashku me Nikolla Zoraqin.

Nga ana tjetër, Rapsodia e Ibrahimit synon të evitojë si akordet minore ashtu edhe ato maxhore, duke shpalosur, (si edhe disa vepra të tjera të tij) një parapëlqim për intervale të përsosura (i 4-ti dhe i 5-ti) me disonanca semitonale. Ka një preferencë natyrale për të shkruarën linare dhe për kontrapunktin në kontrast me homofoninë predominuese të veprave të Daisë, një orkestrim shumë më të komplikuar dhe një ndjenjë kontrastuese shumë më të madhe. Kështu, veprat janë të ndryshme. Por kam përshtypjen se që të dy këta kompozitorë, do të pëlqenin më tepër ta vinin theksin te pikat e përbashkëta në qëndrimet e tyre të kompozimit e sanë diferencat stilistikore. Dhe që të dy veprat duhet të kenë karakteristika specifike dhe jo të përgjithsuara.

P Me krijimtarinë e cilëve kompozitorë perëndimorë do ta krahasonit këtë muzikë?

DAVE Nuk është e lehtë të bësh një krahasim të tillë: është një kulturë muzikore unike, siç e thashë edhe në fillim. Qëndrimi i tyre për zhvillimet harmonike, për shembull. po të mos jesh i mësuar me të, është paksa i veçantë. Edhe tani, për këtë arsye unë e kam të vështirë të ndjek disa nga veprat e Zadesë, ndonëse s'kam asnjë problem me koncertin për piano. Por ndihet ndikimi i romantikëve të shek. 19 dhe 20, veçanërisht siç ndihet edhe ai i disa kompozitorëve sovjetikë. Kjo mund të të lërë përshtypjen se muzika tingëllon e tejkaluar ose anakronike, (veçanërisht me tituj të tillë si "Rapsodi"), por unë do ta kundërshtoja këtë pikëpamje. Baleti i Zoraqit "Cuca e maleve", vë në përdorim teknika të transformimeve tematike mjaft të preferuara nga Listi, por nuk tingëllon fare si një vepër e shek. 19. Një familjarizim më i thellë me veprën e Bartokut duhet të ketë ndodhur kohët e fundit, por unë e ndjej se veprat që e reflektojnë këtë proces mund të jenë shkruar nga pikëpamja e sotme e muzikës dhe historisë së saj. Pasioni dhe heroizmi nuk janë karakteristikë të modës së tashme në shumicën e muzikës evropiane, por ato janë karakteristika mbizotëruese në muzikën shqiptare, si folklorike, ashtu edhe të kultivuar, dhe kjo s'është aspak për t'u çuditur, po të kihet parasysh historia e vendit.

P Na dhatë një tablo fare të detajuar të muzikës shqiptare...

DAVE Zor se mund ta thuash një gjë të tillë. Unë vetëm sa fola në mënyrë të detajuar rreth një pjese të vetme të muzikës koncertale. Dhe ka disa kompozitorë me vlerë si Shpëtim Kushta, Kujtim Laro ose Sokol Shupo, të cilët as që i përmenda. Ju nuk mësuat asgjë për muzikën orkestrale të Ç. Zadesë, simfonitë vokale të Ibrahimit, poemat e vepra të tjera nga Peçi, apo Harapi. Kam dëgjuar të plota shumë pak vepra madhore, si koncerte, simfoni dhe balete, kështu që dikujt, gjatë bisedës, mund t'i kem ngrënë hakun. Ndoshta mund të ketë ndonjë kompozitor që ka shkruar një koncert të shkëlqyer për klarinetë ose për piano e që tani...

— *Drita*, 2 dhjetor, 1990.

ALBANIAN SUMMER: AN ENTERTAINMENT
Album liner note by Dave Smith

Albanian Summer reflects my interest in Albania, its people, their way of life and their music. The country contains some 2 3/4 million people who inhabit an area rather larger than Wales but more mountainous. Their ethnic origins are quite separate from the Greek and Slavic peoples, the language (Albanian) having developed from the old Illyrian language. The history has been one of constant struggle against foreign invaders, usually from neighbouring countries. In the 15th century, the Albanians, under the leadership of their national hero Scanderbeg, kept the Turks at bay for 25 years, thus effectively preventing the Ottoman armies from sweeping into Central Europe. Independence from Turkey was declared in 1912 but Albania's neighbours (Italy, Montenegro, Serbia and Greece) attempted to carve the country up between themselves. Apart from a short-lived democratic government led by Bishop Fan Noli in 1924, the 1920's and 1930's were spent under the dictatorship of King Zog who brought the country increasingly under the influence of Mussolini's Italy. Only in the period since 1944 have the Albanians enjoyed real material, social and cultural progress — no longer is their country the poorest and most backward in Europe. Small wonder, then, that the communist government enjoys an almost unanimous support from its people, something that the British media, for one, is loth to admit.

The Albanian government's adherence to principle rather than compromise hasn't ensured the same popularity internationally. The USA and the Soviet Union are equally condemned as the world's chief perpetrators of military and economic interference and Albania refuses to enter into relations with either. There are no relations with Britain and nor will there be so long as over £20 million of Albanian gold remains in the Bank of England. For their part, the British claim reparations from the so-called "Corfu Channel incident" of 1946, an exercise in gunboat diplomacy that went wrong when two ships entering Albanian waters were damaged by mines laid by another country.

Fortunately, Albania has no such quarrels with British individuals who travel to their country. The fierceness with which they regard their enemies is offset by the abundant hospitality and generosity offered to those who come in good faith. Byron witnessed this national characteristic in 1809. recording his observations in the 2nd Canto of "Childe Harold's Pilgrimage"

> Fierce are Albania's children, yet they lack
> Not virtues, were those virtues more mature.
> Where is the foe that ever saw their back?
> Who can so well the toil of war endure?
> Their native fastnesses not more secure
> Than they in doubtful time of troublous need:
> Their wrath how deadly! but their friendship sure.
> When Gratitude or Valour bids them bleed.
> Unshaken rushing on where'er their chief may lead.

I first visited Albania in 1973 and have returned on several occasions since, usually during the summer (one reason for the piece's title). During these visits I've recorded much music, usually from the radio — folk music, compositions, "light" music and revolutionary songs. The thriving folk music made the deepest impression — perhaps the most surprising aspect is its sheer variety, given the size of the country. The austere homophony of the North contrasts sharply with the rich polyphony of the South: and the oriental colouring of the urban popular music (a legacy of the long Turkish occupation) is quite absent from the music of the countryside (where the Turks never consolidated their grip) Whilst there are obvious similarities with the music of neighbouring areas (Yugoslavia and Greece), some of the differences are quite striking — in general, it can be said that Albanian folk music has a more tenacious quality.

My enthusiasm for the folk music provided the starting point for *Albanian Summer* although my observations of people and places have had a considerable effect on the atmosphere and general flavour. Jan Steele's solo saxophone improvisations had always impressed me throughout the many years I'd known him — I never ceased to be surprised by them although Jan himself seemed to view them as limited in invention. This apparent contradiction brings to mind a memorable description by the late A.L. Lloyd of the "kaba" (which involves the kind of semi-improvisation which opens *Albanian Summer*) — "As with the Blues in the U.S.A., every performance of the kaba is achingly familiar yet always fresh and different." Just before the piece was written, Jan told me that an early inspiration for him as an improviser was A.L. Lloyd's TOPIC record of Albanian folk music...

The piano accompaniment is probably even more difficult than the saxophone part. Both call for players of wider musical background and experience than most concert-artists possess — players, in fact, such as those for whom the piece was written.

The structure of *Albanian Summer* approximates to a combination of classical rondo and variation forms. On the other hand, the variety of styles and rather abrupt juxtapositions of material are similar to those found within (local) Radio Tirana's excellent early-morning folk music programme (it starts at 5.10 a.m. and conveniently lasts for one side of a C90 cassette). By 1980, I was probably most familiar with the orientally-influenced urban popular music and although I wanted *Albanian Summer* to reflect something of the range of music I'd heard in Albania, the work is more biased towards this genre than any other. The listener may detect a fascination with the sound of the typical urban band (usually consisting of clarinet and/or violin, accordion, guitar and drum-kit) — at different times, other instruments such as the gajdë (bagpipe) and çifteli (a 2-string lute) also make an appearance. There is only one short quotation, but a close study of the "common property" of urban music has resulted in my having written melodies which sound familiar to Albanian ears. My presentation of this genre is usually unsophisticated, contrasting with areas of melodic or contrapuntal elaboration with evocations of different genres (e.g., the Eisler-like partisan song). There is not, however, much reference to the music of Albanian composers, little of which I knew at that time. My interest in this area (largely a post-war phenomenon) has been more recent.

Albanian Summer is dedicated to Jan Steele and Janet Sherbourne. It was commissioned with funds made available by West Midlands Arts.

THE MUSIC OF DAVE SMITH
Gavin Bryars, Album liner note for *Albanian Summer,* February 1985.

To even a casual observer of the changing face of English "experimental" music (in the sense of the term coined by Michael Nyman in his book Experimental Music) it is noticeable how frequently Dave Smith's name occurs, and in a wide variety of performing contexts too. A member of the Scratch Orchestra, a member of People's Liberation Music, member of the Smith/Lewis duo, friend and collaborator with Cornelius Cardew, collaborations with John White, founder member of the Garden Furniture Music Ensemble, collaborator with Gavin Bryars, founder member of the English Gamelan. In addition to his performing he has also been very active as a teacher (at Kingsway, Pimlico, Leicester) and he has published important articles — often the first in the field — on Philip Glass, LaMonte Young, the piano sonatas of John White, and, more recently, on new music in Albania. What has perhaps been less noticeable, though not to a more attentive observer, is the evolution of his own composing and the extent to which it follows and sometimes anticipates developments in this area of new music.

I first met Smith in 1971 when he took part in the performance of Christian Wolff's Burdocks at Cecil Sharp House, London, organised by the Scratch orchestra. As far as I know he wrote no music for the Scratch. There are no pieces in any of the published anthologies of Scratch compositions, nor in the collection of improvisation rites. The earliest music of this that I know is systemic in character and grows out of his duo work with John Lewis. This keyboard duo specialised in repetitive music of various kinds — Glass, Riley, Reich, as well as music by themselves and other London-based composers and was active from 1973 to 1978. The American music they played was almost always taken down from recordings since most of it was unpublished (with the exception of some Riley notations that John Tilbury had) and this method of obtaining music that he admires and wants to play is something which Smith continues to use when necessary. His own compositions in this genre were systemic, where any system was employed to create variety within circumscribed limits. He took certain elements from other types of systemic music available. From the music of the Americans he took their interest in modality, but he twisted this by a concentration on a more heavily associative equivalent, "Mode 2" (Messiaen's second mode of limited transposition). From the music of the principle English systemic composers (Hobbs/White duo, the PTO) he took their interest in the combination, in unequal measures, of rigour, allusion and wit. To these two possible references he added his personal highly energetic form of pianistic muscular Christianity, something that has characterised much of his later output (although I suppose that his transcription of Albanian symphonic poems has to count as the atheistic equivalent).

The music from 1977 (some of which was written for the first concert of Garden Furniture music at the AIR Gallery in November 1977) and onwards shows a real awareness of the special characteristics of the performers themselves (as does, say, the music of Duke Ellington). It was his work with the subsequently formed Garden Furniture Music Ensemble that brought Smith to a fuller musical maturity. This ensemble's longish, and happy, life from 1977 to 1979 brought about the close collaboration with John White who has been musical mentor to many composers. In other ensembles associated with White (the Composers Ensemble with William York, Brian Dennis and Roger Smalley; the PTO with Christopher Hobbs, Alec Hill and Hugh Shrapnel), White was always the dominant personality. While this was true to some extent with the GFME, Smith was his artistic equal. His work alongside White revealed a slightly malicious form of humour that had not been apparent in his repetitive work. In his music for the GFME the mixture of 'dirty' chords and allusion provides a wry distortion of much repetitive music. At the same time, a sense of obsession and repetitiveness takes this music away from its sense of the electric. Smith once listed the common musical ancestry of some of this music – Alkan, Weill, Ives, Scriabin, Ellington, Albanian folk music, reggae, Gameian... The frequent exchange of cassettes between members of the group and those on its periphery (Bryars, Ted Szanto) was a way of sharing enthusiasms and of bringing other source materials forward for possible treatment. In some ways almost all of Smith's work epitomises those characteristics of Garden Furniture Music that distinguish it from Satie's original, interior, version – it is "less comfortable, more rough-hewn, and more likely to survive in a hostile environment". Not all the pieces are fast, loud and aggressive it must be said Parts of Indian Spring are quiet and reflective, though they tend to serve as presagers of storms ahead. Other quiet pieces like Instant Coma and Vocalise are certainly soft in dynamics, but have a hard and unsentimental centre.

Between 1973 and 1976 he wrote transcriptions of a number of revolutionary songs which may have seemed like an activity unrelated to the systemic music of the same period. Their common healthy, overt pianistic aggression nevertheless binds them together. Smith has always been interested in the grey area between pure transcription and composition. Liszt, Busoni, Godowsky, Grainger, Sorabji are composers whom he admires immensely. They are all piano virtuosos who wrote, variously, "arrangements", "transcriptions", "pastiches", "paraphrases", "fantasies", "rambles", and much of this moves a long way from its source. The musical concern of this period seems to have been to maintain a shaky and sometimes precarious balance between the "subtle and the blatent" and the works demonstrate a healthy feeling for juicy sonorities and 'dirty' chords.

Smith is not nearly as prolific as White, and there are long periods when he does not compose. Often at these times he makes arrangements and transcriptions for teaching purposes (pieces by Gottschalk, Grainger, Liszt, Busoni, Ellington and Godowsky have all been arranged for student groups at Kingsway and Leicester) and this activity serves the double function of making available the music he loves, and of keeping his ear in good shape. When Nyman wrote Experimental Music in 1972 (though it was published in 1974) he could not have anticipated the direction that English music would take in the 1980's, especially after the death of Cornelius Cardew in

1981. Indeed Smith does not figure in Nyman's book at all. But the French horn player in Burdocks, the astonishing pianist who developed from the Smith/Lewis duo, the ocarina player in National Theatre foyer concerts, the baritone horn player in the AIR Gallery concert, the tenor horn in the GFME, the percussionist in various composer/performer ensembles, the member of the English Gamelan, the occasional bassist in student groups (when they are stuck), has been keenly appreciated by many of us as a musician of rare quality and one of the most interesting composers working in this country. (Apart from Smith, I imagine one could count on the fingers of Paul Wittgenstein's right hand the number of English composers now living — or even not — who have written music in post-war Albania...)

A PICARESQUE STORY
Interview with Jan Steele

Q How did you start the Practical Music label?

JAN It was Janet Sherbourne and I who started it. We wanted mainly to release our own music. We started with *Nobody But You* by Janet Sherbourne, which was an EP, three tracks. Then there was *Albanian Summer*, and then Sherbourne with Mark Lockett did *Slower Than Molasses* (1987), they also did two cassettes, *Walks Abroad* and *Cafe Olé* and they also did two gamelan CD's, the Metalworks' albums *New Gamelan* and *Parrot Soup*. That's all we did. We also released the *Cafecito* album, *El Gato*.

Q How did you come to record the Albanian Summer album?

JAN At the time I was struggling thinking about how I was going to be a saxophone player; because at the time I couldn't see a way of earning with music by playing jazz. The only alternative was playing in shows, which I didn't really want to do. So, I thought I would play classical saxophone, and do concerts. I was trying to commission new repertoire all the time. That was the reason. I have known Dave Smith for several years, and I knew he was a really prolific composer. I asked him to write me a piece. I got some funding from, what was called at the time, the West Midlands Arts, it does not exist anymore. It was a way of distributing government money to the arts; they gave me a commission fee to pay him. That was it. And it was Dave's idea to use Albanian music.

Q So, you did not specifically commission him to do an album based on Albanian music?

JAN No. Just anything, I was happy to have new repertoire, a new piece for saxophone and piano.

Q Were you collaborating with Dave in People's Liberation Music?

JAN I was never involved in any of those things.

Q Neither in Progressive Cultural Association?

JAN No, no. To be honest, I was thinking they are a bit of a joke.

Q Why did you think so?

JAN Well, you know, they were specifically playing music for the workers, and for the Irish who were oppressed by the British. But, the Irish people were never going into their concerts, nor the workers.

Q Why did this happen, what do you think?

JAN Probably they didn't even know about them, possibly they wouldn't go to see them anyway. They would want to go to a country and western concert instead. The problem is that the PLM was a bunch of middle-class musicians. I am sure they were sincere in what they believed, but there was no way this music would ever appeal to the working classes. Maybe one or two people would be interested. During that period I was in London doing a concert, and I ended up going to hospital having my appendix taken out. I was in the hospital for a week, and they said I could go home. On our way to Birmingham with Janet, where we were living at that time, at the station we came across Cornelius Cardew, he was also going to Birmingham. I didn't know him very well, but I knew who he was, and he knew who we were, and he said hello. I was still not feeling very well, but anyway, he sat next to us, and it turned out that he was going back to Birmingham because he was organizing a workers football and contemporary music festival. This must have been sometime in the beginning of the eighties. He told us all about this festival; he was organizing it at Aston University. Now the thing is, I worked for Aston University at that time, where I was programming the music for the arts center, and I never heard anything about this contemporary music and football festival. Although, I did also happen to meet Hugh Shrapnel on a bus. I didn't know him very well, but it turned out he was a music teacher in a school in Birmingham, and he told me a bit more about this festival, and he was really enthusiastic about it. I never saw anything in the press about it, I don't have any idea if it really happened. I am sure, in any case, that they had absolutely no appeal to football fans.

Q   It is easy to predict that.

JAN   I thought they were unbelievably naive, to be honest.

Q   OK. I get that. Were you at that time, like many other contemporary musicians, thinking about the political impact of what you were doing in music? I am referring to your text published in Melody Maker, which offers some sort of Maoist reading of rock music?

JAN   Well, the only reason I wrote that text was to win money in a competition for the best rock writing.

Q   And did you win?

JAN   Yes, I won. I had absolutely no interest in rock music, and barely have it now. But the text was to be about rock music. I was very good at writing garbage. I could be somebody like Plekhanov, or someone like that. I can write about anything.

Q   I understand the rock part of that, but what about the Cultural Revolution, and Mao Tse-tung?

JAN   At that time I just read a book by George Thompson, *From Marx to Mao Tse-Tung: A study in revolutionary dialectics* (1971). Thompson was also a person whose heart was in the right place, but would not mix with workers. He was a professor of Greek at Birmingham University. He was in the Communist Party all his life, as had been his wife, and they were friends of my parents. Anyway, he was one of these people who was disturbed by The Communist Party of Great Britain trying to survive by finding the British way to socialism, and he was also disenchanted with Russia. So, he felt that perhaps the Chinese way to socialism, or Maoist way to socialism would be an answer. He wrote this book with a lot of quotes from Marx, Mao, and Lenin. I happened to read it, and incorporated some of that stuff. Thompson's wife Katherine was a harpsichord player, and she wrote a book about Schubert and Socialism. You know, all these people were living in a fantasy world.

Q   You give the impression that you are not so optimistic about whether musicians or artists in general can engage with workers struggles. But I remember earlier you mentioned a person who successfully bridged these two, music and the left and also did, incidentally, a compilation album on Albania, A. L. Lloyd. Could you tell me more about him?

JAN   I didn't know him very well, but he read my undergraduate thesis on reggae music. I am much more pleased with that than with the essay for *Melody Maker*. I don't think that my thesis on reggae was rubbish at all; it was pretty good. Anyway, my professor of music at York, told me that I should send my thesis to Bert Lloyd. I sent it to him, and he was very interested in it.

He sent it to John Blacking in Belfast. Bert Lloyd came and gave a couple of lectures for the course on World Music I ran at Birmingham University. He just talked about folk music. The thing about him was that he really did come from the working class, he definitely wasn't a middle-class musician, that was for sure. He assisted Ralph Vaughan Wiliams, an excellent British composer. Williams came from a wealthy background, but he was one of these people who were instrumental in the English folk song revival, at the turn of the twentieth century. He was very very successful in Britain, his music was played all the time. *[NB at the moment Vaughan Williams is "composer of the week" on Radio 3 in the UK, and they are running the programme every day for three weeks. It's the 150th anniversary of his birth this year]*. There is a book called the Penguin Book of English Folk Music, compiled by Williams with the assistance of A. L. Lloyd. And then Lloyd went to Bulgaria and Albania and recorded some folk music there. Those recordings were released on the Topic record label, which was basically a communist record label based in Britain. We had quite a few Topic records at home. You know that my parents were communists? They had titles like *My Husband is a Cossack, The Internationale, The Gay Tractor Girls,* a lot of Red Army Choir stuff, and things like that. By the way, Topic records still exist. I don't know if it's a communist record label anymore. It's the oldest independent record label in the world, its eightieth anniversary was in 2019. It started with the Workers' Music Association. There we are!

Q   I guess Lloyd's interest in Albania was not as same as Cardew's?

JAN   No, I very much doubt it. Bert Lloyd was a very sensible guy. He had a realistic attitude to what was possible. He was a member of the communist party, but had a different approach. I remember him talking on radio about his comrade who died during the war, and he had to carry his coffin in the passenger train from Birmingham to London. He did this journey during the night time, a trip lasting for eight hours, which normally would have been only one and half hours.

Q   Apart from Bert Lloyd, could you mention other musicians who were genuinely part of workers' movement, and of leftist politics?

JAN   Well, my general impression is that most musicians I know are at least moderately left wing, I don't know many right wing musicians. People have different ways of expressing their politics; some people get really involved in demonstrations and party activities, some people think their music should reflect their politics. I am really skeptical about that. There are also musicians like Nigel Osborne, who went to Bosnia during the war, and use his music to deal with the children who suffered war traumas. He also worked in Syria. Here is an example of a musician who actually does something with his music, whereas there is no way whatsoever that Cornelius Cardew did anything like that. Probably he would have done it if he had lived longer.

Q   Coming back to the *Albanian Summer*, how was the reception of the album at the time?

JAN   We didn't get many reviews. But we got a lot of invitations to play the piece in concerts. I think we did about 50 performances of it.

Q   Really, where?

JAN   All sorts of places. Music societies in Britain. We did a tour in Germany, a tour in Italy. We played in a festival in Zurich, we played in Vienna.

	Always went really well, wherever we played it.
Q	Were these also political occasions?
JAN	Just concerts. Classical music concerts, generally speaking. The only time ever it was other than that, when we were booked to play in a festival in Vienna, and it was a double bill with an English punk-rock band I had never heard of. We were scheduled to play first, so we were a bit worried that people would throw beer cans at us playing classical music with piano and saxophone. But it turned out that they had to change the order of the programme, because of the noise of punk rock music, so they went first. After the break we went on. I was nervous, but actually we brought the house down. They loved us. We sold a lot of copies of the album.
Q	Why do you think people like *Albanian Summer*?
JAN	Well, it is very melodic. The only people who never seemed to like it were people who were into contemporary music. For them it was not contemporary.
Q	Is the opening section an improvisation?
JAN	Yes, it is semi-improvised. In a sense that Dave gave me some guidelines, some chords. It was supposed to sound like Albanian bagpipe music, the opening.
Q	It is a very eclectic album; how would you describe it?
JAN	Whenever people ask me to write about it for a programme or something, I just say that it is *picaresque*. It is a term from literature, it refers to a particular style of novel, where the hero goes from one incident to another, and the incidents have nothing to do with each other. Don Quixote and Tom Jones are classic picaresque novels.
Q	Could you share more about your musical work before or after this album? You have an album with John Cage?
JAN	No, I haven't been working on John Cage's music. The only reason is that for the album, *Voices and Instruments* (Obscure, 1976), Brian Eno decided to put us on other sides of the same album. So, the John Cage side has nothing to do with me.
Q	Ok, now I got it.
JAN	Many people think that I collaborated with John Cage, but I didn't. I didn't meet him either.
Q	What were your musical interests in the seventies and in the eighties?
JAN	Anything I was interested in. Always has been. I was brought up in European Classical Music tradition, and still I am very heavily into it. I was into Béla Bartók, but into jazz as well. To a certain extent I was into pop music. I was involved in a pop group called The Copy. It was a completely different experience. When you are in classical or jazz music, you rehearse and perform. If you leave the band no one would care about it, you would be replaced by someone else. Whereas in a pop group, if you do a gig with another band, they would think you are deserting the group. And also pop music rehearsals seemed to take so much time, compared to other types of rehearsals. Also, it was too loud for me. I did not listen to pop music until 1970, when I was twenty, and I didn't listen to it much. Enough to familiarize myself with a few things.
Q	So mostly classical and jazz?
JAN	Yes, but I got also involved in Indian pop music. Purely by accident to be honest. I met a guy called Mangal Singh who ran my local off-licence, and whose daughter went to school with my son. It turned out he was one of

the leading Indian pop music singers in Britain. I started playing with this band *Chirag Pehchan*. One thing led to another, and I ended up playing in some 25 or more Indian albums. This was the start of the Bhangra boom, that is a Panjabi folk music played mostly on western instruments. It became a big thing in Britain from about 1980. It still is a big thing. I joined that band when it started to become successful. When I say successful it is not successful in the sense that we were touring around the world. We were doing more dinner dances, weddings, etc. The most interesting part for me was recording albums. I co-wrote two albums. I arranged strings on a couple of other albums.

Q   Do you earn your living by playing music?

JAN   Well mostly by teaching. The gig situation is up and down. During covid there were no gigs. Before that it was not going particularly well. Now I do a gig about once a week.

Q   Where are your gigs?

JAN   Nowadays I mostly do jazz functions. The last one I did was a wake, which is what we call here a party after a funeral. Before that I played at a wedding. This Saturday I will be playing at an eightieth birthday party. Two weeks later I am playing at a garden party. Mostly saxophone with a jazz quartet. I would like to focus more on composing, I am 71 now, and I can not foresee that I will be able to perform indefinitely. But I need some spare time for composition.

Q   Wouldn't it be great to re-release an *Albanian Summer* album?

JAN   We are definitely going to re-record it this summer. We just had a new album released by Community Library, *Distant Saxophones*. Includes both old archival records and new re-arrangements. But yes, let's re-record *Albanian Summer* again. Question is whether we are too old for it. The saxophone part is not so hard, but the piano part is very very hard.

    I wish I would have more time to dedicate to creating music. Possibly only if I would sell the house, then I would have money. I don't have a large enough pension to be able not to teach. I have to work in my retirement time.

Q   I guess that is related to the music and class background that we were talking about at the beginning?

JAN   Yes. Also, composing takes a lot of time for me. Dave, for example, can easily compose stuff. I wish I could do that. But I just sit down and agonize over it.

Q   Is there anything you would like to add, especially about Albanian Summer?

JAN   Well, I have never been to Albania, the interest was mainly in the music. One thing, the times when we were recording the album the conditions were terrible, it was really awful. It was a new studio which was set up at Birmingham University, where we recorded it. They had a very good piano, Steinway. The problem was that they did not have a suppressor on the power supply, and there were electric spikes on the recording. So, we would record the take, and it would go really really well, and the engineer would say stop, there was a spike. It was like that for two days. It was sickening. Not the best conditions. We didn't have enough money to go to a proper studio.

Q   How many copies were printed?

JAN   A thousand.

Q	How come Gavin Bryars wrote liner notes for the album?
JAN	Well, Dave worked with Gavin over the years. They have always been very close. Dave went to work in Leicester Polytechnic (now De Montfort University), which is where Gavin was head of music. I know Gavin but not particularly well. He has this very ironic way of writing. To be honest, I would not write sleeve notes like that, but I thought it would be useful because he was famous. I actually remember only one review of the album, which was published in a Birmingham arts newspaper. I remember the reviewer being really angry about Gavin making that joke about Paul Wittgenstein.

Arts Report, October, 1985

Smith: Albanian Summer (Jan Steele/Janet Sherbourne) Practical 2

by Christopher Morley

DAVE SMITH'S 'entertainment' *Albanian Summer* was composed in 1980 with funds made available by West Midlands Arts and dedicated to Jan Steele and Janet Sherbourne, a Sutton Coldfield-based duo who have since performed it to great acclaim at various locations both in this country and abroad. They recorded it in 1984, and it is one of the most exciting releases I have heard for a long time.

Albanian Summer is the result of several visits made by Smith since 1973 to that tiny country, a fascinating meeting-point of many different cultures and traditions and one which barks so xenophobically at the tainted outside world. In it the composer displays his acute observation of the variety of folk-styles thrown up by the interaction of Albania's history and geography, and the endearingly naive looseness of the structure of this vast 41-minute duo for alto saxophone and piano is unified by Smith's utter commitment to the recreation of the spirit of the country's music.

Jan Steele's saxophone is an ideal vehicle for the evocation of the sound of the near East, his jazz inflections wailing out microtones which are immediately exotic; this is how the piece begins, with a semi-improvisatory 'kaba' on the sole instrument, eventually joined by an oscillating ostinate low down on the piano. From here we are suddenly into a march á la Kurt Weill in its angularity and strutting accompaniment, leading us into a tapestry of moods and aural impressions exhilarating and reflective by turns.

One influence has already been mentioned, and there are many others. In his valuable background note Dave Smith gives a formidable roll-call of composers and transcribers, but I feel this is a mistake, leading the sharp-eared listener to spot others who have not been cited: I heard Satie (a 'Gnossienne'), Liszt, Enesco, inevitably Bartok in his Bulgar moods, and, I suspect, Skalkottas. These all employ an oriental lingua franca, and quotations from them, subconsciously assimilated, do nothing to detract from the integrity of this heart-warming work.

Steele and Sherbourne perform with dignity and dedication, the latter's clarity of articulation and subtle pedalling creating an atmosphere of plaintive mysteriousness, the range of piano textures often reflecting the obsession of turn-of-the-century French composers with Eastern sonorities.

The side-break comes at a natural point, an explosive piano cadenza rumbling onto an ominous pause; the record turns over, the saxophone picks up the keyboard's mournful thread and the music develops into a lengthy, impassioned threnody, and I must confess to being quite sad when the ensuing wild, skirling dance brought this lovable creation to a close.

Engineered by Jonty Harrison at Birmingham University, mastered and pressed by Nimbus, the recording is vivid and immediate, with pristine surfaces (there is, however, a slight drop in level after a couple of minutes — nothing serious). Smith's own interesting sleeve-note has to share space with a surely unwittingly obscurantist appreciation of the composer by Gavin Bryars, leaving an unpleasant aftertaste with its concluding cruel joke at the expense of the one-armed pianist Paul Wittgenstein.

Albanian Summer will be performed at The Triangle, Gosta Green by Jan Steele and Janet Sherbourne at 1pm on October 31st. Their artistry is beyond doubt: prepare to be impressed by their stamina as well!

New Music

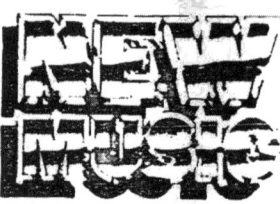

Life goes on after 'the death of experimental music as we have known it': in particular the composer Dave Smith has encountered an Albanian Summer, which Keith Potter introduces

THE ENGLISH composer Dave Smith, like George Nicholson and Walter Zimmermann, was born in 1949. At the end of this month, on May 30, a 45-minute (yes *45-minute*) piece for alto saxophone and piano, commissioned with funds from West Midland Arts, is to be given its first performance at Birmingham Arts Laboratory by Jan Steele and Janet Sherbourne, for whom it was written. It might also be noted that the English Gamelan Orchestra, of which Smith is a member, is giving a concert in the QEH on May 18 as part of the English Bach Festival — on which *Upbeat* will be reporting in the next issue.

Of my three forty-niners, Nicholson's music has sprung fairly directly from the world of the post-war avant-garde, though as I explained before, his use of expressive consonance, even of tonality, has been rethought in the light of Pousseur's thinking on these matters. Zimmermann's approach to simple consonant materials has come via Satie and Cage and an attitude that is commonly referred to as 'experimental' rather than avant-garde.

Smith's background is also a an experimental one: he was in the Scratch Orchestra; he became involved with the political debate which led to and continued long after the orchestra's demise, and he has made some very fine and quite virtuosic piano arrangements of music by Cardew and Eisler and also of Albanian revolutionary songs; with his fellow composer and pianist John Lewis he did much to make Philip Glass's earlier repetitive music known in this country and composed a number of systemic works himself; then for nearly two years he was a member of John White's group Garden Furniture Music which played non-systemic tonal music composed entirely by its members.

Since Garden Furniture Music's demise around two years ago, Smith has written very little music, at least in comparison with his pretty prolific output in the immediately preceding years. Whatever suggestion of crisis there may be in this, and to what extent it is due to the Death of Experimental Music as we have known it, may be at least partly allayed by the new piece, written, incidentally, for performance in the city in which he was born and brought up.

Entitled *Albanian Summer* and composed last year, the work is described by Smith as an 'entertainment'. Its bewildering allusions to many different turn-of-the-century styles of Western composition (a feature which his recent music shares with that of John White), and to jazz and to Jan Steele's style of free improvisation in a broadly 'free jazz' context in particular, are unified by the all-pervading influence of Albanian folk music. Smith became familiar with the music of Albania from his regular trips there; he first went in 1973, only a few years after Westeners were first allowed to visit' a communist country which, situated between Yugoslavia and Greece and largely cut off by mountains, is generally regarded here as remote, hostile to the outside world and underdeveloped.

The use of Albanian folk sources has led Smith towards a fresh discovery of melodic and harmonic elements which integrate surprisingly well with his other concerns. The styles of vocal and instrumental embellishment to be found in this music are also an important influence on the piece, which includes scope for saxophone improvisation within clearly defined limits reflecting not only Smith's Albanian involvement but also Albanian folk music's influence on Steele's regular style of improvisation.

Smith also wishes *Albanian Summer* to draw attention to Albania itself, since he believes that its political system has much to teach the West (he points, for instance, to the fact that there has been no inflation there for many years). Like Cardew, Smith believes that a composer can and should do something to reflect his political beliefs in his music. His present tonal style, which many would regard as merely conservative, is a result, however, not of political concerns alone but of a belief in direct and expressive communication in music which, unlike, he feels, that of most avant-garde-influenced composers, manages to remain unobsessed with technique for technique's sake.

> In the next issue:
> the making of an
> English Gamelan
> Orchestra

Classical Music, May 2, 1982

NEWSLETTER. AUGUST 1985

*IT'S "RECORD REVIEW" TIME!
AS SYLVIA HALLETT TAKES A SPIN WITH A BRAND NEW DISC....*

ALBANIAN SUMMER by DAVE SMITH

Played by JAN STEELE (alto sax) and
JANET SHERBOURNE (piano)

I don't own many records for a musician, but it just happens that my personal favourite for several years has been a record of Albanian music, so it was with great delight that I heard that Dave Smith's 'Albanian Summer' has now come out. My memory of the live performance I heard some time ago was of music which employs a high degree of skill and technique, requiring oodles of stamina to tell an exciting musical story exploring all the extremes of emotion. Listening to the record, my memory is confirmed, but furthermore the listener is wafted into a curious travel agents where the journeys are not only spatial but also temporal; visits to Ravel, Rachmaninoff, Debussy, Bartok, Weill are all ones that I spotted, although the accompanying publicity mentions Lili Boulanger, Percy Grainger, Alkan, Sorabji, Cage, Godowsky, Gershwin, Ives and Ellington. These influences are served up as side-dishes to the anticipated Albanian main course. One might think this an odd combination but Dave Smith manages to glide gracefully from one reference to another without ever losing his own stylistic integrity. Incidentally, I might add that he performed recently at the LMC in Michael Parsons' "Expedition to the North Pole." Jan Steele and Janet Sherbourne have performed in previous LMC festivals, and like Dave Smith have a foot in various musical camps, as sampled in their other records "Voices and Instruments" (Obscure) and "Nobody But You" (Practical).

Albanian Summer begins with an ear-rending wail from the saxophone - excellent opener if ever I heard one, compelling you to listen further. After a n undeniably Albanian-sounding opening section using the tremolo drone and passionate ornamented melody, the music turns towards Bartok and Ravel regarding the harmony and treatment of folk material; but just as I am thinking how classical this all sounds on such a well-tuned piano, the sax enters with a march in its raucous lower register, followed by some high piercing phrases initating the sound of a shawm, and then into a softer clarinet sound (very beautiful). The music even flirts with fugue and shows us some impressive slides on the sax (I think it must be hard to bend the notes so much on a keyed instrument). Towards the end of side one there's some pretty impressive tremolo piano imitating the sound of the cymbalum or mandolin, while the sax plays very fast passages which sound very difficult and has you sitting on the edge of your seat, wondering whether the driving rhythm is going to fall apart - but it never does! It is lovely to be able to listen to sound in a sensuous way - the last chord on the piano is held down until the sound has completely faded. Indeed, I feel this piece fully explores the different timbre possibilities afforded by the two instruments.

Side two puts the listener into a melancholic mood with a lopsided rhythm and floating melody which is sometimes played upside down upon itself like a reflection in a lake. Filmic scenes of East European barren landscapes flit across my mind. The music becomes mysteriously calmer where most other composers would have started to build a climax - calm-before-the-storm effect - and, sure enough, it erupts into... Rachmaninoff? Debussy?... The next rippling passage is what reminded me most of my Albania record, an ever-twisting and turning section of ornamentation, sinuous and ear-teasing. More assymmetrical rhythms and compelling tunes lead us up to a reprise of some themes at the end of side one.

My friend, Liz, stood at the door while I was listening to the record - "What is this music? It's really nice... I feel really touched by it" - and she took down the details with the intention of buying it. The next time I attempted to listen to it on my own another friend dropped by and asked "What is this?" and remarked "It's beautiful."

SYLVIA HALLETT.

ALBANIAN SUMMER - PRACTICAL 2.
Distributed by Nine-Mile distribution, Lower Avenue, Leamington Spa, Warwickshire, 0926-881211, through The Cartel.
Practical Music are at 502 Chester Rd, Sutton Coldfield, West Midlands, B73 5HL.
021-350 2320.
Record retails at around £5.49.

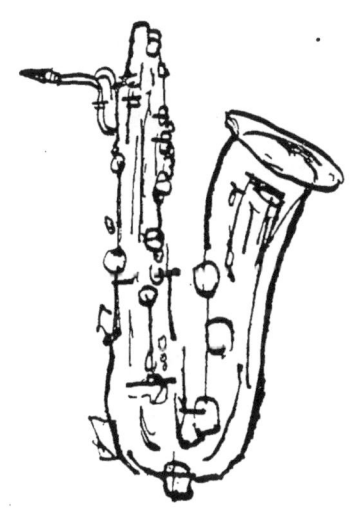

Waterlogged Albanian summer

Sutton Coldfield saxophonist Jan Steele plans to record what is possibly the longest ever work written for a solo wind instrument.

Albanian Summer is a 45-minute epic for alto saxophone and piano written in 1980 by Birmingham composer Dave Smith, who now teaches music in London and at Leicester Polytechnic.

The work was performed for the first time by Jan and his wife, Janet Sherbourne, at a Birmingham Arts Lab concert last May. And in the next few months, they will be taking the classical work to various British venues starting in Northern Ireland this week with performances at the Ulster Polytechnic tomorrow and Queen's University, Belfast, on Thursday.

"It is the best saxophone work I have come across—a remarkable piece of music," Jan, who lives in Chester Road, Sutton Coldfield, told me.

"It is a vigorous, romantic, rhythmic and melodic *tour de force* inspired by Albanian folk music. But unlike other compositions inspired by folk music, this work avoids any tendency to sentimentality.

"I do get breaks from playing during the work but performing the piece does take a lot of stamina. My lip tends to get sore and my reed tends to get waterlogged."

Jan, who is 31, is now planning to tape the work at Birmingham University's Elgar Concert Room on February 7 so it can be released on record.

"Albania's national radio station, Radio Tirana, want to play the work," he explained. "If no recording companies are interested in the tape, we will bring it out ourselves as a record."

She's punchy

Our Picture Desk had a request for some boxing photographs the other day from the *Irish Independent*.

"Who is that calling," asked our man. "Mary Punch," replied the Irish paper's London correspondent.

Outlook black

We may think of the French as pragmatic and sceptical; but a glance at any church bookstall in France will give another impression of them as a nation deeply involved in religious and moral controversy.

We can continue our investigation of them under this guise at an exhibition of modern French books on religion which opens at Birmingham University today.

The books will deal with many aspects of religion in France: Roman Catholicism, Protestantism, Orthodoxy, Judaism etc. It will be on view in the University Library between 10 a.m. and 4 p.m. Monday to Friday for two weeks.

In connection with the exhibition there will be a series of lectures on the same subjects at the Extra Mural Department at Winterbourne where such themes as "The Church in France today", Georges Bernanos and Pierre-Emmanuel will be discussed.

Let us hope the books and the lectures do not confirm another

JOHN BRIGHT

22
RECORD REVIEW

"ALBANIAN SUMMER" by Dave Smith, played by

Jan Steele (alto saxophone)
Janet Sherbourne (piano)

Reviewed by Moira Brillo

Having spent several summers in Albania, Dave Smith is undoubtedly the British composer with the most profound knowledge of Albanian folk music. This forty-five minute continuous "entertainment" (as the composer calls it) is in no way a medley. It is an "Albanian study", a recreation for British ears of the essence of this vivid folk music for two instruments, with the occasional touch of nostalgia and anger here and there. The piano does as percussion, plucked strings and even at times the human voice. The alto saxophone recalls the violin, clarinet and surle, but represents something of a compromise. Nevertheless, it is hard to imagine any other composer capturing his subject with greater realism, using only these two instruments.

Dave Smith provides a few clues on the sleeve of the record, but for me the value of the work would be greatly enhanced if he were to issue a "Short Guide", perhaps including extracts from the score, which could make clear the intricacies of construction. But, as someone said: "Why understand, just listen!"

("Albanian Summer" is recorded on a long-playing (33 rpm) disc obtainable from:

Practical Music,
502, Chester Road,
Sutton Coldfield,
West Midlands,
B73 5HL

at the special price of £4.70, including postage, for members of the Albanian Society).

Midland saxophonist Jan Steele with his wife Janet Sherbourne—making a long record. See *Waterlogged Albanian summer*.

Birmingham Post, Jan 18th, 1982

Albanian Life, No 33, 1985

ZiZ! (Janet Sherbourne and Jan Steele) press materials

ALBANIAN MUSIC

at Midlands Arts Centre, Canon Hill Park, Edgbaston

on Sunday, May 4th, 1986 at 7.30 p.m.

PROGRAMME

1. Tish Daija : Poem for Violin (1968)

   Tish Daija, who works in the Institute of People's Culture in Tirana, is one of several Albanian musicians born in the 1920s. He was responsible for composing (in 1953) the first Albanian string quartet and (in 1963) the first Albanian ballet Halil and Hajrija
   The Poem for Violin, often performed with orchestral accompaniment, is usually presented with the title Dite te gezuara (Happy Days) - which, according to the composer, is incorrect. The title seems to have stuck, however, since it is perfectly in agreement with the character of the piece, particularly in the faster sections, which display a strong folk-dance element.

2. Pjetër Gaci : Violin Concerto (1959)

   Pjetër Gaci is himself a violinist, although he is perhaps better known as a composer.
   This work is the earliest Albanian concerto and offers a particularly clear example of the juxtaposition of classical and folk styles. The first movement (allegro agitato) shows an unashamed awareness of the 19th century repertoire - albeit with a strong East European flavour. The third movement (a sonata-rondo) is equally unashamedly folk inspired, using as its main theme an authentic dance melody from Kukes in the north-east of the country. The slow second movement is a marriage between the polarities - a slow, lyrical romance.

3. Thoma Gaqi : Borova (1972)

   In the summer of 1943, German troops invaded Albania - replacing the Italian forces as occupiers. Albanian partisans inflicted heavy losses on the Nazis in their first encounter. In revenge, the Germans destroyed the village of Borova (in south-east Albania), killing all the inhabitants. Thoma Gaqi's symphonic poem is tragic-heroic in tone and reflects the courage and heroism of those who struggled against the invaders. Folk songs are not quoted - and a western listener could be excused for missing out on the features of Southern Albanian folk music that are present. Gaqi is one of the leading composers of the younger generation and Borova is one of his earliest acknowledged works.

INTERVAL

4. Dave Smith : Albanian Summer (1980)

   Albanian Summer was occasioned by the composer's fourth visit to Albania in August 1980. In so far as the piece reflects an interest in Albania, its people and their music, it should be noted that Albanian culture (unlike that of Britain) possesses a strong national identity and is permeated with the ideals of social progress. The thriving folk music, which has a more tenacious quality than that of neighbouring countries, makes a particularly strong impression and the piece makes liberal use of the "common property" of Albanian music (particularly the urban folk music), although only one intentional quotation appears. The work is in one movement and lasts approximately 45 minutes.

   Albanian Summer was commissioned with funds made available by West Midlands Arts: it is dedicated to Jan Steele and Janet Sherbourne.

* * * * * * * * *

The performers will be, in the first half, Dave Smith (piano) and Alexander Balenescu (violin) and, in the second half, Janet Sherbourne (piano) and Jan Steele (alto saxophone).

At the invitation of the Amnesty International group at Oxford University, the Secretary of the Albanian Society, Bill Bland, will speak on

HUMAN RIGHTS IN ALBANIA

at 1 p.m. on Wednesday, June 18th, 1986 at St. John's College, Oxford.

Members of the Albanian Society are welcome to attend.

The Albanian Society seeks to foster friendship between the peoples of Britain and Albania. Membership is open to all who support this aim and costs £4.00 each year. This includes the subscription to our journal 'Albanian Life' which is produced every four months.

If you would like further information about the Albanian Society, please contact:

   Dr.J.Puntis,
   Secretary Midlands Albanian Society,
   52 Rookery Road,
   Selly Oak,
   Birmingham B29 7DQ

Midlands Arts Centre, Albanian Society concert, programme notes, 1986

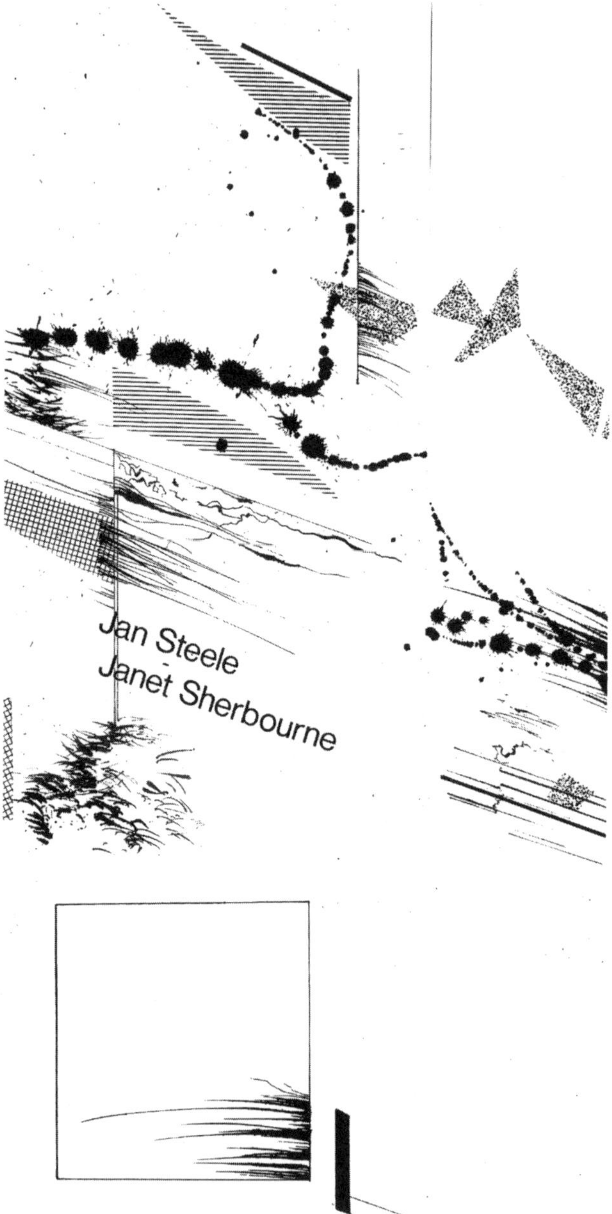

Jan Steele
Janet Sherbourne

Requirements
Tuned concert grand piano or good quality upright.

A studio recorded demonstration cassette tape is available on request.

Fees 1982/3 season £150 plus expenses of travel and accommodation where applicable

1983/4 season £175 plus expenses of travel and accommodation where applicable

All enquiries to
502 Chester Road
Sutton Coldfield
West Midlands
B73 5HL
021-350 2320

A brochure of Jan Steele and Janet Sherbourne's works

Barber Institute of Fine Arts
25 November

JANET SHERBOURNE
(voice and piano)

JAN STEELE
(alto saxophone)

Sonata (1937) for alto saxophone and voice   BERNHARD HEIDEN

Heiden was born in Frankfurt in 1910 and has lived in the USA since 1935. He studied with Hindemith at the Berlin Hochschule für Musik from 1929 to 1933. His last appointment was as Chairman of the Composition department at Indiana University.

This sonata of three movements, dedicated to the great American saxophonist, flautist and teacher Larry Teal, the founder of straight saxophone playing in the USA, was probably the first 'classical' composition of non-French origin to become established as a repertoire piece for the instrument. It clearly reflects the composer's Germanic origin, not least the influence of his teacher, Hindemith.

North Wind (1970), for solo saxophone   HOWARD SKEMPTON
first performance

Howard Skempton was born in Chester in 1947. He studied composition privately with Cornelius Cardew and was instrumental, with Cardew and Michael Parsons, in founding the Scratch Orchestra, the large mixed-media performance group which became the prime focus of experimental music in England. Since 1974 he has worked in a duo with Michael Parsons, performing music based on rhythmic systems for percussion duo, voices, piano and other instruments. He has recently completed a commission (his first) for the Merseyside Youth Orchestra, *Chorales*, and is currently working on a piece for the Omega Guitar Quartet and on a collection of songs for Janet Sherbourne and Michael Parsons.

Skempton's compositions are all miniatures, displaying an outward simplicity which hides a disciplined internal structure. Like the works of Morton Feldman, who is an important influence, they present unusual performance difficulties, because the sparse texture reveals the slightest lack of control. *North Wind* is no exception to this general description. It was written in March 1970 for Michael Parsons, who was playing curved soprano saxophone at that time. Skempton has given his permission for the piece to be performed on any saxophone.

Jan Steele

Folksong(s) for solo voice, and
Ballads for voice, saxophone and piano

Interval

Albanian Summer (1980), for alto saxophone   DAVE SMITH
and piano
Commissioned by Jan Steele and Janet Sherbourne with funds made available by West Midlands Arts

Dave Smith's background is an experimental one. He was in the Scratch Orchestra; he became involved with the political debate which led to and continued long after the orchestra's demise, and he has made some very fine and quite virtuosic piano arrangements of music by Cardew and Eisler and also of Albanian revolutionary songs; with his fellow composer and pianist John Lewis he did much to make Philip Glass's earlier repetitive music known in this country and composed a number of systemic works himself; then for nearly two years he was a member of John White's group Garden Furniture Music, which played non-systemic tonal music composed entirely by its members.

Since Garden Furniture Music's demise around two years ago, Smith has written very little music, at least in comparison with his pretty prolific output in the immediately preceding years. Whatever suggestion of crisis there may be in this, and to what extent it is due to the Death of Experimental Music as we have known it, may be at least partly allayed by the new piece, written, incidentally, for performance in the city in which he was brought up.

Dave Smith himself writes:

"*Albanian Summer* is the second of a series of extended 'seasonal' works and was occasioned by the composer's fourth visit to Albania in August 1980. In so far as the piece reflects a strong interest in Albania, its people and their music, it should be noted that Albanian culture (unlike that of Britain) possesses a strong national identity and is permeated by the ideals of social progress. The thriving folk music, which has a more tenacious quality than that of neighbouring countries, made a particularly strong impression and the piece makes liberal use of the "common property" of Albanian music although only one intentional quotation appears. The work is in one movement and lasts approximately 45 minutes."

The bewildering allusions in the work to many different turn-of-the-century styles of Western composition (a feature which his recent music shares with that of John White), and to jazz and to Jan Steele's style of free improvisation in a broadly 'free jazz' context in particular, are unified by the all-pervading influence of Albanian folk music.

Keith Potter

Barber Institute concerts, 1981

Autumn 1981

BARBER CONCERTS

Wednesday at 8

Barber Institute of Fine Arts
University of Birmingham

CONCERT

A concert of Albanian music was presented at Canterbury College of Technology on Friday, October 4th as part of the Canterbury Festival. The concert suggested something of the variety of Albanian music through urban folk music, a symphonic poem and partisan and revolutionary songs.

The urban music included well-known songs (e.g., "Lule malësore", "A kan' ujë ata burime", "Artizane e Lumës") and instrumental numbers (e.g., "Valle festivale" and two kabas) such as one would hear by a small band playing in an Albanian café. These were performed by Ian Mitchell (one of England's most distinguished clarinettists), Adrian Lee (guitar), Dave Smith (piano) and Wally Cardew (percussion).

Also in the programme were a piano transcription of Thoma Gaqi's symphonic poem "Borova" and a varied selection of Albanian songs presented by the Progressive Cultural Association. The evening concluded with a rendering of "Enver Hoxha, tungjatjeta".

The Albanian Society had organised in the hall the photo-exhibition "40 Years of Socialist Albania", together with a bookstall/information bureau. A number of new members joined the Society.

The meeting on November 24th will be preceded at 2.45 p.m. by a brief Members' Meeting.

Nominations for the Committee of the Society should be sent to the Secretary to reach him by November 20th.

The meeting will be followed in the evening in the same hall by a social which will include refreshments, videos and music.

Albanian Life No 33, 1985

A Concert of Albanian Music

On November 1st, 1984 the Progressive Cultural Association organised a concert of Albanian music in London, interpreted by Dave Smith (piano) and Alex Balanescu (violin).

The programme consisted of:

Symphonic Poem : "Borova" . . Thoma Gaqi (arr. Smith)
Trio . . . . Limos Dizdari
Violin Concerto . . . . . Pjetër Gaci
  (first performance in Britain)
Poem . . . . Tish Daija
  (first performance in Britain)

The concert was preceded by a talk on "Composers in Albania" by Dave Smith.

Day School on Albania

On Saturday, December 8th, 1984 the Albanian Society, in conjunction with the University of Birmingham, held a day school on Albania at Winterbourne, Birmingham.

The morning session was taken by Professor Martin Smith, President of the Society, on "Albania, Ancient and Modern".

In the afternoon, Bill Bland, Secretary of the Society, lectured on "The Albanian Economy", and Dr. John Puntis, Midlands Secretary of the Society, on "International Perspectives", with special reference to the Corfu Incident of 1946.

All the lectures were illustrated with visual aids. The school was full, and the discussions after each lecture were lively and constructive.

Albanian Life, No 31, 1985

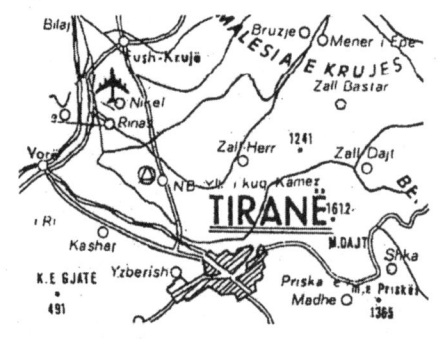

A flyer for the concert of ZiZ! in West Berlin, 1987

QUEEN'S UNIVERSITY MUSIC SOCIETY

Thursday 21 January 1982

at 1.15 p.m.

in the Harty Room

JAN STEELE (saxophone), JANET SHERBOURNE (piano)

* * *

Albanian Summer

for alto saxophone and piano

"*Albanian Summer* is the second of a series of extended 'seasonal' works and was occasioned by the composer's fourth visit to Albania in August 1980. In so far as the piece reflects a strong interest in Albania, its people and their music, it should be noted that Albanian culture (unlike that of Britain) possesses a strong national identity and is permeated by the ideals of social progress. The thriving folk-music, which has a more tenacious quality than that of neighbouring countries, made a particularly strong impression and the piece makes liberal use of the 'common property' of Albanian music although only one intentional quotation appears. The work is in one movement and lasts approximately 45 minutes."

(Dave Smith)

"Entitled *Albanian Summer* and composed last year, the work is described by the composer as an 'entertainment'. Its bewildering allusions to many different turn-of-the-century styles of Western composition and to jazz and to Jan Steele's style of free improvization in a broadly 'free jazz' context in particular, are unified by the all-pervading influence of Albanian folk music. Smith became familiar with the music of Albania from his regular trips there; he first went in 1973, only a few years after Westerners were first allowed to visit a communist country which, situated between Yugoslavia and Greece and largely cut off by mountains, is generally regarded as remote, hostile to the outside world and underdeveloped.

The use of Albanian folk sources has led Smith towards a fresh discovery of melodic and harmonic elements which integrate surprisingly well with his other concerns. The styles of vocal and instrumental embellishment to be found in this music are also an important influence on the piece, which includes scope for saxophone improvization within clearly defined limits reflecting not only Smith's Albanian involvement but also Albanian folk music's influence on Steele's regular style of improvization.

Smith also wishes *Albanian Summer* to draw attention to Albania itself, since he believes that its political system has much to teach the West. Like Cardew, Smith believes that a composer can and should do something to reflect his political beliefs in his music. His present tonal style, which many would regard as merely conservative, is a result, however, not of political concerns alone but of a belief in direct and expressive communication in music which, unlike, he feels, that of most avant-garde-influenced composers, manages to remain unobsessed with technique for technique's sake."

Keith Potter

Jan Steele & Janet Sherbourne

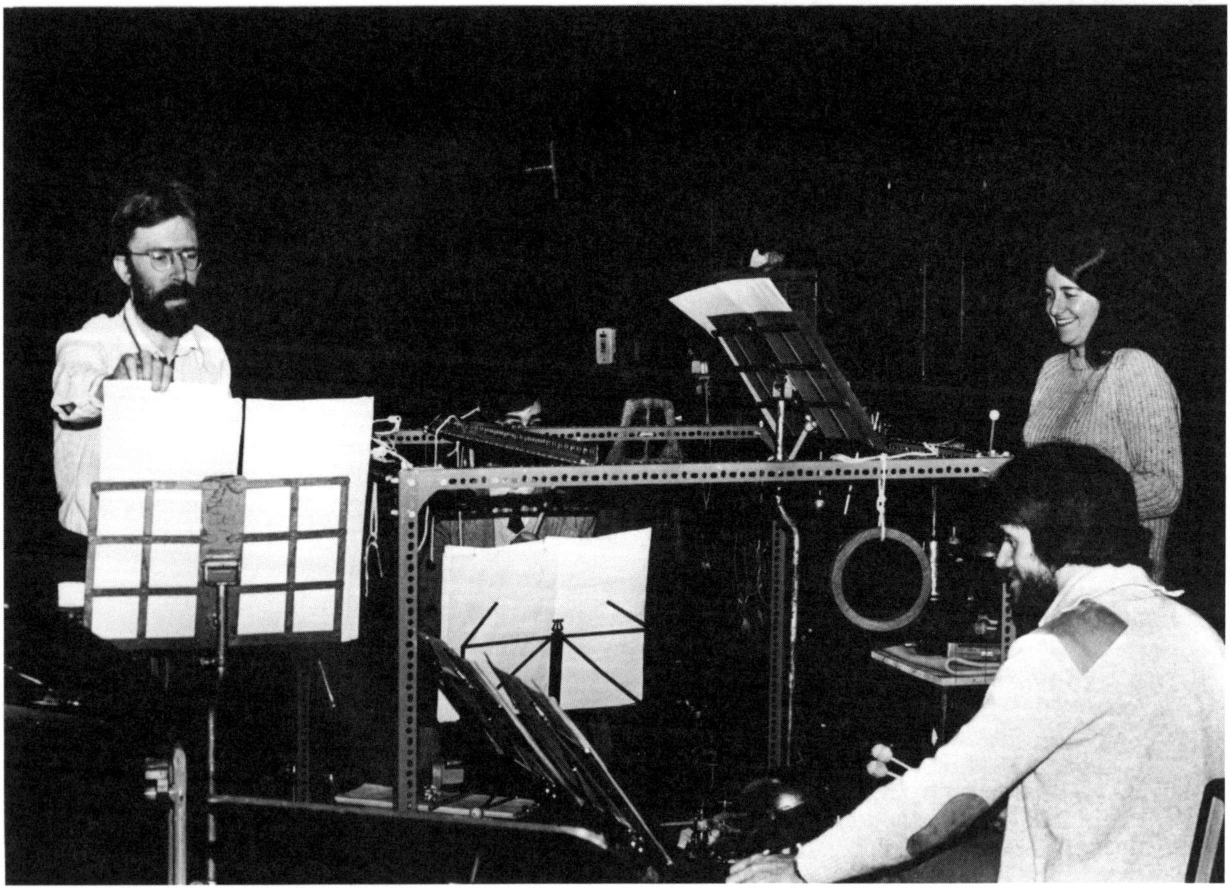

Jan & Janet & colleague Kevin Edwards,
Centre For The Arts, Aston University, around 1979

The annotated bibliography of foreign language books published by '8 Nëntori'. This is only a slice of the vast amount of books published in many different languages in socialist Albania. The bibliography also includes publications by local Marxist-Leninist branches in Turkey, Norway, Sweden, and Finland, in their own languages.

Our main reference was the bibliography on Albania compiled by William B. Bland, published by Clio Press in their World Bibliographical Series (Vol. 94) in 1988.

THE ALBANIAN PEOPLE HAVE BEEN AND ARE WITH THE JUST CAUSE OF THE PEOPLES

Speech of the head of the delegation of the PSR of Albania at the 32nd session of the General Assembly of the UNO

ENVER HOXHA

THE CRISIS OF ITALIAN MODERN REVISIONISM

ENVER HOXHA

KHRUSHCHEV KNEELING BEFORE TITO

(September 13, 1963)

ENVER HOXHA

PROLETARIAN DEMOCRACY IS GENUINE DEMOCRACY

THE ALBANIAN PEOPLE HAVE BEEN AND ARE WITH THE JUST CAUSE OF THE PEOPLE

Nesti Nase. Tirana: 8 Nëntori, 1977.
22p. 16,5 × 11,7 cm.

Reproduces the speech made by the then Albanian Foreign Minister at the General Assembly of the United Nations in October 1977. Nase surveys the world situation as seen by the Albanian government and denounces the superpowers — the United States and the Soviet Union — for their threats to peace and the independence of nations. He also describes Albania's foreign policy, in particular its full moral support for all people struggling for their national independence and social advancement.

THE CRISIS OF ITALIAN MODERN REVISIONISM

Enver Hoxha. Tirana: 8 Nëntori, 1977.
64 p. 17,8 × 11,4 cm.

Contains two writings of Enver Hoxha, the first published in *Zëri i Popullit* (The People's Voice) in November 1964. The second was written in 1962 and published in Volume 24 of the *Selected Works*. Hoxha criticises the Italian revisionist ideas headed by Palmiro Togliatti's posthumous publications as well as the thesis of the 10th Congress of the Communist Party of Italy.

KHRUSHCHEV KNEELING BEFORE TITO

Enver Hoxha. Tirana: 8 Nëntori, 1977.
25p. 17,5 × 11,3 cm.

This article was first published in the newspaper *Zëri i Popullit* (The People's Voice) on September 13, 1963 and is a useful illustration of the changed view of the Soviet Union which was then held by the Albanian government. It condemns Khrushchev for "rehabilitating" the Yugoslav leader, Josip Broz Tito (1892-1980), and claims that this illustrates the Soviet leadership's departure from Marxist-Leninist principles.

PROLETARIAN DEMOCRACY IS GENUINE DEMOCRACY

Enver Hoxha. Tirana: 8 Nëntori, 1978.
40p. 17,4 × 11,3 cm.

The text of a speech Hoxha made to the General Council of the Democratic Front of Albania in September 1978. He discusses the operation of 'proletarian democracy' in Albania, and maintains that this is far more democratic than the 'parliamentary democracy' of capitalist states.

NUK KA LIRI TË VËRTETË SHOQËRORE PA EMANCIPIMIN E PLOTË TË GRUAS

Tirana: Naim Frashëri, 1967.
155p. 19,8 × 13,2 cm.

There will be No Real Social Freedom Without the Full Emancipation of the Women, includes letters from women workers and peasants from all around Albania addressed to Enver Hoxha, written in the first half of 1967. It also includes the excerpts from Enver Hoxha's greetings to them, from which some were published earlier in the periodicals *Zëri i Popullit* and *Bashkimi*. The letters cover the progress in the emancipation process of women, the political and social role of women in the construction of socialism, the fight for the liquidation of the old patriarchal traditions, the struggle against commodification of women, elimination of unnecessary expenses of banquets, etc. The workers and peasants who wrote the letters span from the voluntary brigades from all over the country to the women collectives in cooperatives to the local women organisations of villages and towns.

OUR POLICY IS AN OPEN POLICY, THE POLICY OF PROLETARIAN PRINCIPLES

Enver Hoxha. Tirana: 8 Nëntori, 1974.
80p. 14 × 10 cm.

A speech delivered at the meeting with the electors of the Tirana No. 209 precinct, on October 3, 1974. The first part of the speech reviews the economic progress in Albania and contrasts it with the unemployment, inflation, and economic crises afflicting the capitalist world. Enver Hoxha characterises the political systems in the West as 'sham democracy', cites the coup in Chile in support of this contention, and asserts that true democracy exists only in Albania. The second part of the speech consists of a review of the international situation as seen from Tirana, including the situation in Cyprus, Palestine, the People's Democratic Republic of Korea, and Cambodia.

DVADESET PET GODINA BORBE I POBEDA NA PUTU SOCIJALIZMA

Enver Hoxha. Tirana: Naim Frasheri, 1970.
69p. 16,4 × 11,6 cm.

The Serbo-Croatian translation of a speech by Enver Hoxha was delivered at a meeting in November 1969 to commemorate the twenty-fifth anniversary of the liberation of Albania from Italian and German occupation. Hoxha provides the official view of the economic and social progress made by Albania since 1944, emphasises that the Party of Labour of Albania will not deviate from Marxist-Leninist principles, denounces the Soviet military intervention in Czechoslovakia, and declares that the socialist revolution will ultimately triumph throughout the world, although the struggle will be a protracted one.

CHINESE WARMONGERING POLICY AND HUA KUO-FENG'S VISIT TO THE BALKANS

Tirana: 8 Nëntori, 1978.
22p. 16,5 × 12 cm.

This editorial from the newspaper *Zëri i Popullit* (The People's Voice) published in September 1978 provides a clear view of the then strained relations between Albania and China. It denounces the visits of the Chairman of the Central Committee of the Communist Party and the Premier of the State Council of China, Hua Kuo-feng to Romania and Yugoslavia as "an act of provocation against Albania" and accuses China of expansionist aims in the Balkans, of seeking to become a superpower, and of seeking unity with the United States to attain "the domination of the world".

NUK KA LIRI TË VËRTETË SHOQËRORE PA EMANCIPIMIN E PLOTË TË GRUAS

TIRANË, 1967

ENVER HOXHA

OUR POLICY IS AN OPEN POLICY, THE POLICY OF PROLETARIAN PRINCIPLES

ENVER HOXHA

DVADESET PET GODINA BORBE I POBEDA NA PUTU SOCIJALIZMA

CHINESE WARMONGERING POLICY AND HUA KUO-FENG'S VISIT TO THE BALKANS

Editorial of the newspaper «Zëri i popullit», organ of the Central Committee of the Party of Labour of Albania September 3, 1978

ЭНВЕР ХОДЖА

РЕЧИ, БЕСЕДЫ, СТАТЬИ
1969-1970

ENVER HOCA

Çu En-lay ile Konuşma

HALKIN BİRLİĞİ YAYINLARI

ZERİ I POPULLIT

DEVRİMİN
TEORİ ve PRATİĞİ

★★★

KOMÜN YAYINEVİ

PROLETARIANS OF ALL COUNTRIES, UNITE!

ENVER HOXHA

IMPERIALISM AND THE REVOLUTION

TIRANA, 1979

РЕЧИ, БЕСЕДЫ, СТАТЬИ (RECHI, BESEDY, STAT'I) 1969-1970

Enver Hoxha. 8 Nëntori, 1980.
448p. 16,5 × 12 cm.

Speeches, Conversations, Articles is the Russian translation of Hoxha's book *Against Contemporary Revisionism*, originally published in Albanian in 1979. A collection of articles, statements, speeches, and transcripts of discussions analysing the international aspect of Brezhnevist revisionism, which Hoxha was criticising as the "social imperialism".

ÇU EN-LAY İLE KONUŞMA

Enver Hoxha. Istanbul: Halkın Birliği Yayınları, 1977.
36p. 18,6 × 12,8 cm.

Turkish translation of *Conversation with Chou En-lai*. The text of Hoxha's statement of Albania's view of the international situation was made to Chinese Premier Chou En-lai (1898-1976) during the latter's visit to Albania in March 1965. The statement had remained unpublished until 1977.

DEVRİMİN TEORİ VE PRATİĞİ

Istanbul: Komün Yayınevi, 1977.
30p. 19,5 × 13 cm.

The Theory and Practice of the Revolution appeared in the daily newspaper *Zëri i Popullit* (The People's Voice) on 7 July, 1977 and expressed Tirana's first public criticism of the theory of 'three worlds' being put forward by Peking as the basis of China's foreign policy. It condemns the authors of the theory, without naming them, as 'anti-Marxist-Leninist' and 'counter-revolutionary' and reaffirms the loyalty of the Party of Labour of Albania to Lenin's analysis of imperialism and to Stalin's thesis that the world is divided into two camps — of imperialism and socialism.

IMPERIALISM AND THE REVOLUTION

Enver Hoxha. Tirana: 8 Nëntori, 1979.
464p. 19 × 13 cm.

In this book, which was first published in Albania in April 1978, Hoxha amplifies and makes an explicit analysis of the world situation made the previous year in an editorial in *Zëri i Popullit* (The People's Voice) entitled 'The theory and practice of the revolution'. Here he openly denounces the Chinese leaders as "revisionists" and Mao Tse-tung Thought as "an anti-Marxist theory". The book concludes with a condemnation of "revisionism of all hues", that is, of "Chinese revisionism" and equally its Soviet, Yugoslav and Eurocommunist variants. Apart from versions in different languages, which were published by *8 Nëntori* (November 8), the book was translated and published by a myriad of independent Marxist-Leninist parties in the US, Canada, Turkey, Finland, Sweden, the UK, and elsewhere.

EUROCOMMUNISM IS ANTI-COMMUNISM

Enver Hoxha. Tirana: 8 Nëntori, 1980.
291p. 20,2 × 14 cm.

In this work, Hoxha characterises the ideology of the Spanish, French and Italian communist parties — which the Spanish communist leader Santiago Carillo refered as 'Eurocommunism' — as "a new variant of revisionism". Hoxha points out that Eurocommunism has rejected the Marxist-Leninist doctrine of the need for revolution and the dictatorship of the proletariat, and spreads the "illusion" that socialism can be attained through peaceful, parliamentary means. He acknowledged that the Eurocommunists justify NATO and support the presence of US troops in Western Europe and concludes that Eurocommunism is, in fact, a repudiation of communism.

THE KHRUSHCHEVITES

Enver Hoxha. Tirana: 8 Nëntori, 1980.
484p. 19,8 × 13,5 cm.

Written in 1976, this book provides an official Albanian interpretation of the country's relations with the leaders of the Soviet Union from the death of Stalin in 1953 to the Soviet rupture of relations in 1961. There are chapters on the 1956 Congress of the Communist Party of the Soviet Union (which Hoxha attended), when Khrushchev launched his denunciation of Stalin, and on the crisis in Hungary in the same year.

THE ANGLO-AMERICAN THREAT TO ALBANIA

Enver Hoxha. Tirana: 8 Nëntori, 1982.
446p. 19 × 13 cm.

Considers the relation of Albania with Britain and America from the 19th century to the 1960s. The book is mostly concerned with the Second World War period and, Hoxha expresses forcibly the view that the Western Powers attempted to sabotage Albania's War of National Liberation in an effort to secure a pro-Western regime in Albania after the end of hostilities. This view is continued in the author's account of the Corfu Channel Incident, the question of the Albanian gold and the Anglo-American attempts to overthrow the post-war regime in Albania between 1949 and 1954.

THE SUPERPOWERS: 1959-1984: EXTRACTS FROM THE POLITICAL DIARY

Enver Hoxha. Tirana: 8 Nëntori, 1986.
678p. 21,5 × 14,9 cm.

This is the last work of Hoxha, published posthumously. In it, he equates the Soviet Union, characterised as a country in which capitalism has essentially been restored, with the United States. They are both, Hoxha claims, aggressive, expansionist superpowers that are "the arch-enemies of the people". He also analyses the conflicts of interest between the superpowers and the role of the rival military blocs — the Warsaw Pact and NATO.

Historia til Arbeidets Parti i Albania

ENVER HOXHA
Kvinnefrigjering i Albania
3 ARTIKLAR 1967–1972

Arnavutluk Emek Partisi M.K. ve Arnavutluk Hükümetinin Çin Komünist Partisi M.K. ve Çin Hükümetine
MEKTUBU

HALKIN KURTULUŞU YAYINLARI

Zeri i Popullit
SOSYAL-EMPERYALİZM ÜZERİNE

günce yayınları

HISTORIA TIL ARBEIDETS PARTI I ALBANIA

Institute of Marxist-Leninist Studies. Oslo: Oktober, 1976.
510p. 20,8 × 14,6 cm.

This, the second edition of the history of the Party of Labour of Albania extends the range of the earlier edition to 1980 and makes some amendments. In particular, the former favourable view of the Communist Party of China and the assessment of China as 'a bastion of socialism and a powerful base of the world revolution' have been refuted.

KVINNEFRIGJERING I ALBANIA: 3 ARTIKLAR 1967–1972

Enver Hoxha. Forlaget Oktober: Oslo, 1977.
47p. 20,7 × 14,6 cm.

Norwegian translation of Enver Hoxha's three speeches on the emancipation of women in Albania. Includes: 'About some aspects of the issue of women in Albania (1967)', 'Everyone must understand what rights and freedoms women and young people have, and be involved in keeping them together (1969)', and 'On promoting socialist-democracy in the family (1972)'.

ARNAVUTLUK EMEK PARTİSİ M. K. VE ARNAVUTLUK HÜKÜMETİNİN ÇİN KOMÜNİST PARTİSİ M. K. VE ÇİN HÜKÜMETİNE MEKTUBU

Istanbul: Halkın Kurtuluşu, 1978.
50p. 19 × 13,2 cm.

Turkish translation of the letter of the CC of the Party of Labour and the Government of Albania to the CC of the Communist Party and the Government of China. It is the letter from Tirana to Peking, dated 29 July 1978, in reply to the Chinese note of 7 July announcing the decision to cease economic and military aid to Albania and to recall its economic and military experts from that country. The letter denounces the action as a "brutal, perfidious and hostile act", insists that Albania has always pursued correct state relations with China, and attributes China's action to the fact that Albania was unwilling to accept China's foreign policy as its own.

SOSYAL-EMPERYALİZM ÜZERİNE

Istanbul: Günce Yayınları, 1977.
178p. 18,5 × 13 cm.

On Social Imperialism covers texts compiled from *The Party of Labour of Albania in Battle with Modern Revisionism* (Tirana, 1972) and *The Congress of Capitalist Restoration and Social Imperialism* (Tirana 1971). The selected texts include a critical open letter from 1964 addressed to the Communist Party of the Soviet Union, texts about modern revisionisms, a critique of Soviet Union's Social-imperialism "disguised as proletarian internationalism", and "the senile disease of rightism" in European workers and communist movements, etc.

YUGOSLAV 'SELF-ADMINISTRATION': A CAPITALIST THEORY AND PRACTICE

Enver Hoxha. Tirana: 8 Nëntori, 1978.
101p. 18 × 11,2 cm.

Presents a historical study of Yugoslavia since the Second World War as seen from an official Albanian perspective. Hoxha analyses in some detail the economic system in contemporary Yugoslavia and concludes that it is a disguised form of capitalism.

REVİZYONİZM VE MACERACILIK YENİLGİYE, MARKSİZM-LENİNİZM ZAFERE GÖTÜRÜR

Enver Hoxha. Istanbul: Aydınlık Yayınları, 1975.
123p. 19,4 × 13,2 cm.

Revisionism and Adventurism Lead to Defeat, Marxism-Leninism to Victory brings Enver Hoxha's Report to the 6th Congress of the Party of Labour of Albania from November 1971 and his speech delivered on October 3, 1974, at the meeting of electors of the No. 209 precinct in Tirana. The first text covers the international situation, Albania's foreign politics, and Marxism-Leninism in Albania. The second text contains the economic and political developments and the country's foreign politics.

THE TITOITES: HISTORICAL NOTES

Enver Hoxha. Tirana: 8 Nëntori, 1982.
643p. 22,3 × 15,5 cm.

Describes the relations between Albania and Yugoslavia, mainly between 1941 and 1981. More than 500 pages are dedicated to the tense confrontations between the two countries until the political and diplomatic split in 1948. Hoxha considers the clash with Yugoslavia as their first fight with modern revisionism in which 'the Titoite spider-web had been spun' even inside the Albanian communists. Hoxha is very sympathetic towards his early ally Miladin Popović. He remembers Popović as a supporter of Albanian self-determination against the expansionist ambitions of 'Tito and his cliques'. Hoxha provides the first full official details of the charges of treason made against former Prime Minister, Mehmet Shehu (1913-81), who, it is stated, committed suicide to avoid disgrace and prosecution. The content also provides information regarding the charges levelled against the members of Shehu's family.

EMEK PARTİSİ VE ANTİ-REVİZYONİST MÜCADELE

Enver Hoxha. Istanbul: Yöntem Yayınları, 1976.
296p. 19,3 × 12 cm.

The book is a compilation of texts, speeches, annual resolutions, annual reports of the Party of the Labour, and letters written by Enver Hoxha. The documents range from 1948 to 1961 and were originally compiled by Patrick Kessel along with his introduction text for the French translation *Les Communistes Albanais Contre Le Révisionnisme: De Tito à Khrouchtchev, 1942-1961*.

ENVER HOXHA

YUGOSLAV "SELF-ADMINISTRATION" A CAPITALIST THEORY AND PRACTICE

ENVER HOCA

Revizyonizm ve Maceracılık Yenilgiye, Marksizm-Leninizm Zafere Götürür!

Arnavutluk Emek Partisi'nin Altıncı Kongresine Rapor
ve
Tiran'ın 209 Nolu Seçim Bölgesi Seçmenleriyle Konuşma

AYDINLIK YAYINLARI

ENVER HOXHA

THE TITOITES

Emek Partisi ve anti-revizyonist mücadele

ENVER HOCA
AEP-MK. kararları

DRITA SILIQI

PROBLEMET E GRUAS NE SHTYPIN E LUFTES NACIONAL-ÇLIRIMTARE

Mehmet Şehu

MİLLÎ KURTULUŞ SAVAŞININ TECRÜBESİ ve MİLLÎ ORDUMUZUN GELİŞMESİ ÜZERİNE

günce yayınları

THE 8th CONGRESS OF THE WOMEN'S UNION OF ALBANIA

ENVER HOCA

ARNAVUTLUK EMEK PARTİSİ VII. KONGRE RAPORU

★★★
Komün Yayınları

PROBLEMET E GRUAS NË SHTYPIN E LUFTËS NACIONAL-ÇLIRIMTARE

Drita Siliqi. Tirana: 8 Nëntori, 1979.
140p. 16,4 × 11,3 cm.

Problems of Women in the Press of the National Liberation War reviews the role of the women organisations and their political and literary activities during the Antifascist National Liberation War. It reveals how the first antifascist women organisations were established in Albania and how they approached the oppression and emancipation of the Albanian women in the newly formed illegal press of communists. The second part of the book contains the reproductions and excerpts of some of the important texts about the subject written in this period and published in newspapers and journals such as *Bashkimi, Kushtrimi i Lirisë, Liria, Gruaja Shqiptare,* etc.

MİLLİ KURTULUŞ SAVAŞININ TECRÜBESİ VE MİLLİ ORDUMUZUN GELİŞMESİ ÜZERİNE

Mehmet Şehu. Istanbul: Günce Yayınları, 1977.
100p. 19,5 × 13 cm.

Turkish translation of Mehmet Shehu's book: *On the experience of the national liberation war and the development of our national army*. The original (1947) report republished here, put forward the Communist Party of Albania's case for rejecting Yugoslav advice on the military organisation. The four-part report deals respectively with: the conception and development of the National Liberation Army; the experience of the War of National Liberation; the comparison between a partisan and a regular army; and military operations in the terrain of Albania. The report concludes that Albania's army should be organised based on the experience gained during the War of National Liberation, that it should be a "People's Army" which has mastered the art of "People's War" and that it should be under the leadership of the Communist Party.

THE 8TH CONGRESS OF THE WOMEN'S UNION OF ALBANIA

Tirana: 8 Nëntori, 1978.
157p. 16,5 × 11,5 cm.

Contains texts of the speeches from the 8th Congress of the Women's Union of Albania held between 1st to 4th of June, 1978 in Durrës. The subject is the emancipation of women and their role in the socialist construction of the country. Includes texts by Enver Hoxha, Lenka Çuko — the Alternate member of the Political Bureau of the CC of the PLA, Vito Kapo — President of the General Council of the Women's Union of Albania, as well as many greeting texts by 23 international delegations spanning from Vietnam to Chile.

ARNAVUTLUK EMEK PARTİSİ VII. KONGRE RAPORU

Enver Hoxha. Istanbul: Komün Yayınları, 1976.
247p. 19,3 × 13,2 cm.

This is the report of the Central Committee of the Party of Labour of Albania submitted by Hoxha to the 7th Congress of the Party in November 1976. It covers the report on the new constitution, development of the economy, the leading role of the Party in the complete construction of socialist society, the international situation and the foreign policy of the PRA, class struggle and the education of the working masses and 'the struggle against modern revisionism.

REFLECTIONS ON CHINA

Enver Hoxha. Tirana: 8 Nëntori, 1979.
2 vols. 784p. + 814p. 22 × 15,5 cm.

This book is made of excerpts of Hoxha's political diary. The first volume covers the period between 1962 and 1972 and the second between 1973 and 1977. It presents a picture of the Albanian leader's increasing disquiet with the actions and policies of the leaders of China — with the Cultural Revolution, the extreme cult of personality built up around Mao, Chinese secrecy and pressure, and with China's rapprochement with Yugoslavia and the United States. The final excerpt, dated December 26, 1977, sketches the history of the Communist Party of China; characterised as "revisionist", while Mao Zedong is described as "not a Marxist-Leninist" and the Chinese Revolution as, not a socialist revolution but "a bourgeois-democratic revolution of a new type."

LA CONTRE-RÉVOLUTION DANS LA CONTRE-RÉVOLUTION: A PROPOS DES ÉVÉNEMENTS DES ANNÉES 1980-1983 EN POLOGNE

Spiro Dede. Tirana: 8 Nëntori. 1983.
313p. 18,5 × 11,7 cm.

French translation of the counter-revolution within the counter-revolution. Presents the official Albanian view of events in Poland in the period between 1980 and 1982. The author's main conclusions are that the crisis in Poland at this time was due to the abandonment of Marxist-Leninist principles and genuine socialism by the Polish leadership. Moreover, it is claimed that the revolutionary movement directed against the Polish state came under the leadership of right-wing forces because of the absence of the leadership of a genuine Marxist-Leninist party. Resonates with Enver Hoxha's thesis that the Solidarity movement is a syndicalist bourgeois counter-revolution within the larger social-imperialist counter-revolution of Poland and the Warsaw Pact.

REFLECTIONS ON THE MIDDLE EAST: 1958-1983

Enver Hoxha. Tirana: 8 Nëntori, 1984.
550p. 19,5 × 12,6 cm.

These are extracts from the political diary published in different instalments. Here Hoxha makes a detailed analysis of the Middle East, the hotbed of conflict in the seventies and the eighties. The book deals with the Middle Eastern strategies of the United States and the Soviet Union; the role of Israel; the struggle of the Palestinians for a national homeland; the history and present role of Islam; the Cyprus question; the Soviet intervention in Afghanistan; the character of the revolution in Iran; and the significance of oil. Particularly interesting is a historical sketch of Arab culture. The observations with continuing relevance.

ALWAYS IN THE VANGUARD OF SOCIETY, BEARER OF PROGRESS

Ramiz Alia. Tirana: 8 Nëntori, 1989.
57p. 18 × 11 cm.

Includes the speech given by Ramiz Alia at the 8th Plenum of the CC of the PLA. Alia talks about the task of the party against the current troubles encountered during the socialist construction of Albania. He says that the grave situation is the result of "current international developments", including the imperialist violence in the Middle East, political and economic crisis in Yugoslavia, Gorbachov's perestroika, etc.

Enver Hoxha
Reflections on China

Spiro Dede
La contre-révolution dans la contre-révolution
Les événements de Pologne (1980-1983).
L'abandon du marxisme-léninisme.
La revanche de la dialectique. «Solidarnosc».

TIRANA 1983

ENVER HOXHA
REFLECTIONS ON THE MIDDLE EAST

RAMIZ ALIA
ALWAYS IN THE VANGUARD OF SOCIETY, BEARER OF PROGRESS

ALBANIA
TIEDOTE 1/81

COMITE NATIONAL DES VETERANS DE LA GUERRE DU PEUPLE ALBANAIS

CHANTS RÉVOLUTIONNAIRES

ALBANIA
TIEDOTE 1974 No 2

IULK. SUOMI - ALBANIA SEURA

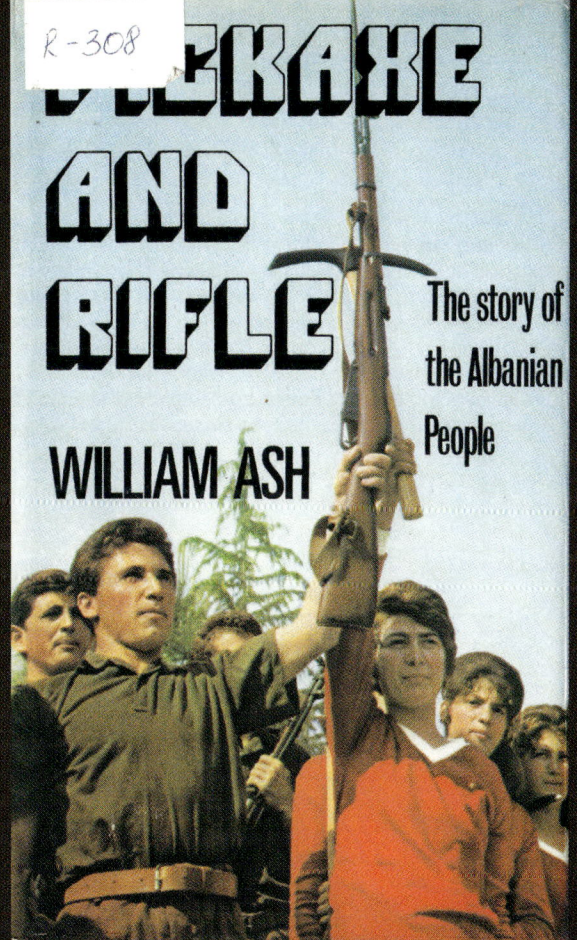

PICKAXE AND RIFLE
The story of the Albanian People
WILLIAM ASH

ALBANIA TIEDOTE, NO. 1, 1981

Helsinki: Suomi-Albania Seura, 1981.
18p. 21 × 15 cm.

Brings the review of Enver Hoxha's article collection, an article on the trade politics of Albania, Albanian films, touring exhibition of Albanian paintings in Finland, information about learning Albanian, and arrangements for travel to Albania.

ALBANIA TIEDOTE, NO. 2, 1974

Helsinki: Suomi-Albania Seura, 1974.
32p. 30 × 21 cm.

The second issue of *Albania Tiedote* (Albania Information) published by the Finnish-Albanian Society. The Society was founded in 1971 by people who were involved in Helsingin marxilais-leniniläisen seuran (HMLS, Helsinki Marxist-Leninist Society). Translations, Albania journey reports, news, and activities of the Society. Favourite slogan of the journal: "When the class speaks, bureaucracy is silent" ("Kun luokka puhuu niin byrokratia vaikenee").

CHANTS REVOLUTIONNAIRES

Tirana: 8 Nëntori, 1974.
90p. 18,3 × 13 cm.

Includes a compilation of Albanian revolutionary songs with notations translated into the French language. The tunes were sung during "demonstrations, in prisons, before the firing squad or the gallows". In addition to revolutionary songs by Albanian composers, this volume also includes patriotic songs, as well as world revolutionary melodies, to which the writers have given new content by adapting them to the language.

PICKAXE AND RIFLE.

William Franklin Ash. London: Howard Baker, 1974.
271p. 22 × 13,5 cm.

After considering the history of Albania from the earliest times, Ash, an American who was born in 1917 and who was a BBC script editor until his retirement in 1980, provides an account of post-Second World War Albania which is sympathetic to the present regime. For example, he depicts Albania as "a genuinely free society". The book describes the functions of the state, the role of the Party of Labour and the mass organisations; the economy; arts and culture; the health service; and family relations. Chapter fifteen provides background information about the breach of relations with the Soviet Union in 1961.

ALBANIA DEFIANT

Gun Kessle and Jan Myrdal. New York and London: Monthly Review Press, 1976.
185p. 20,7 × 14 cm.

This is a very sympathetic account of Socialist Albania and a thorough analysis of its political history. The authors see the very existence of Socialist Albania as a challenge to Washington but also to Moscow, Rome and Belgrade. After analysing the long history of oppression against the worker and peasant Albanians, the disillusionment caused by Balkan social democrats and the struggle for independence and socialism, the authors go on to examine the political cleavages after the Second World War and the construction of Socialism in the country.

ALBANIA TODAY: POLITICAL AND INFORMATIVE REVIEW, NO. 2 (69), 1983

Tirana, 1983.
64p. 25,5 × 21,5 cm.

Selected papers from the commemorative meeting on the 100th anniversary of the death of Karl Marx. Review of Enver Hoxha's book *The Titoists*, and the translation of a long article from the daily *Zëri i Popullit* (The People's Voice), titled 'Fresh Testimony of the Anti-Albanian Policy of the Yugoslav Leadership'.

ALBANIA TODAY: POLITICAL AND INFORMATIVE REVIEW, NO. 3 (64), 1982

Tirana, 1982.
64p. 25,5 × 21,5 cm.

Albania Today was a bimonthly political review, published in English, French, German, Spanish, and Italian. This issue includes an article by an international law specialist Arben Pluto, who argues, through the historical overview, that the Albanian question is rather the question of a national movement than a diplomatic question. It also brings a long review of Enver Hoxha's The Anglo-American Threat to Albania, and the lengthy analysis by Kolë Prenga, lecturer at the University of Tirana, with a slogan-like title, 'International Monopolies — Tools of Economic and Political Expansion'.

ALBANIA TODAY: POLITICAL AND INFORMATIVE REVIEW, NO. 6 (73), 1983

Tirana, 1983.
80p. 25,5 × 21,5 cm.

Among the subjects, which the scientific conference has covered, it contains the Marxist-Leninist theory of the revolution, the socialist economy, the dictatorship of the proletariat and the class struggle in Albania, the ideological and cultural revolution, defence of the socialist homeland, the foreign policy of the Party of Labour of Albania, and the struggle against modern revisionism.

ALBANIAN LIFE

No. 5 (New series)
Autumn 1977

Contents

p. 2   The Albanian theatre
p. 4   Speech of the Albanian delegate to the General Assembly of the United Nations (Oct. 1976), cont.
p. 7   The origins of the Albanian people
p. 8   The folklore: wealth of the Albanian people
p. 11 Report of the Central Committee of the Party of Labour of Albania (extracts)
p. 23 Education of the school youth in Albania
p. 27 Andon Zako Çajupi (1866-1930)
p. 30 The exploitation of the Albanian peasant at the beginning of the 20th century
p. 37 The extension of the health service

ALBANIAN LIFE

No. 16 (New Series)
November 1980

CONTENTS

ALBANIAN FOLK DANCES : Ian Price . . . . . . p. 1
TWO SHORT STORIES : Nonda Bulka . . . . . . p. 6
THE EVOLUTION OF REALISM IN ALBANIAN LITERATURE : Koço Bihiku (Part 2) p. 9
THE DEVELOPMENT OF OUR ENERGY : Lazar Papajorgi . . . . p. 12
FROM THE ALBANIAN COOKERY BOOK: Byrek me Presh (Leek Pie) . . . p. 13
"DEAD MAN'S QUEST" (An Old Albanian Legend) . p. 14
FIVE POEMS : Aleks Çaçi . . . . p. 16
ALBANIA ANCIENT AND MODERN : Martin B. Smith p. 19
RADIO TIRANA : Broadcasts in English . . . p. 21
HOLIDAYS IN ALBANIA . . . . p. 21
THE SEVENTH FIVE YEAR PLAN : Ilia Dedi . . p. 23
ALBANIAN CHROME : Kope Kyçku . . . . . . p. 23
"CHILDE HAROLD" : A poem by Ismail Kadare . p. 24
FOUR NEW ALBANIAN FEATURE FILMS . . . . . p. 25

ALBANIAN LIFE

Special Issue
August 1979
No. 11
(New Series)

Contents

Enver Hoxha:
"NOTES ON CHINA", Volume I: 1962-1972

(being an abridged translation of:
"Shënime për Kinën", Volume 1;
Tirana; 1979).

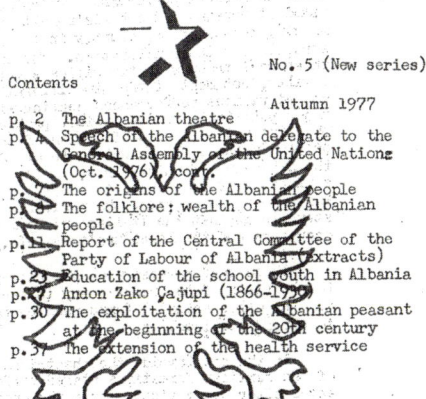

ALBANIAN LIFE

50p

Quarterly Journal of the Albanian Society
New Series, No. 18   July 1981

ALBANIAN LIFE NO. 5, AUTUMN 1977

London: The Albanian Society, 1977.
39p. 22 × 14,8 cm.

The issue opens with a short text on Albanian theatre, followed by the speech of Resi Malile, the Albanian delegate to the General Assembly of the UN, defending the independence of Cyprus, freedom of Palestine, and condemnation of the South African Apartheid regime. The article on folklore defines it as "a collective work of the masses through the centuries". The closing article, 'The exploitation of the Albanian peasant at the beginning of the 20th century', is a translation from the summary of the article in *Studime Historike, No. 3*, 1975. The author analyses the base of the entire Ottoman fiscal system underlining the parasitical character of the colonial plunder, which the bourgeoisie of the independent Albanian state adopted.

ALBANIAN LIFE NO. 16, NOVEMBER 1980

Ilford: The Albanian Society, 1980.
26p. 22 × 14,8 cm.

The main piece of the issue is Ian Price's essay 'Albanian Folk Dances', which gives a basic introduction to the thematic and regional specificities of Albanian dance. Argues that during the National Liberation Struggle and in the years of socialism, the folk dances have gone through transformation, now including mixed groups of male and female dancers. The short note to the essay tells that Ian Price has traveled extensively in the Balkans and the Middle East, however, his main interest is Albania, which he has visited on several occasions. He is the musical director of the AVAZ Folk Ensemble based in Los Angeles. The issue also includes a receipt for baking Leek Pie (Byrek me Presh).

ALBANIAN LIFE NO. 11, AUGUST 1979

Ilford: The Albanian Society, 1979.
34p. 22 × 14,8 cm.

The entire issue is an abridged translation of Enver Hoxha's 'Shënime per Kinën', Volume 1, published that year in Tirana. They are taken from the first volume of a new work by Hoxha entitled 'Notes on China', which is composed of extracts from the political diary kept by the writer during the period from 1962 to 1972, years when Albania started to have strong relations with China until the US President Richard Nixon visits Beijing, which was protested by Albania. This is part of several translations included in *Albanian Life* dealing with the radical break of Albania with China in 1978, which was the main subject of Marxist-Leninist organisations worldwide. The backpage announces the upcoming lecture of A.L. Lloyd on the polyphonic folk music of Albania, and an eye-witness account of the recent earthquake which struck Northern Albania.

ALBANIAN LIFE: QUARTERLY JOURNAL OF THE ALBANIAN SOCIETY, NEW SERIES NO. 18, JULY 1981

Ilford: The Albanian Society, 1981.
64p. 22 × 14,8 cm.

This is the first issue of the new series of *Albanian Life*, announcing that it will be published quarterly from now on instead of three times a year. The issue begins with a comment by Anastas Kondo on a painting — 'The Joan D'Arc of Albania' — which is believed to be painted by Ndoc Martini in 1911 in Paris. The other texts covers topics such as the nationalisation of banks in Socialist Albania, Beethoven and French Revolution by Fan Noli, the pension system in Socialist Albania, Social Environment in Charles Dickens, an exposure of *The Daily Mirror*'s falsified news on Albania, as well as a short story by Nasi Lera and a poem by Rezear Xhaxhiu called 'Stalin City'. The issue also includes a declaration of an Albanian Society meeting held in London, opposing repressions by Yugoslav authorities in Kosovo.

ALBANIAN LIFE: QUARTERLY JOURNAL OF THE ALBANIAN SOCIETY, THE SPECIAL CONGRESS ISSUE, NO. 20, FIRST QUARTER 1982

Ilford: The Albanian Society, 1982.
64p. 21 × 14,8 cm

This is the special issue dedicated to the 8th Congress of the Party of Labour of Albania held in Tirana from November 1st to 7th, 1981. It covers a summary of the report on the activity of the Central Committee presented by Enver Hoxha and a summary of the economic report presented by Mehmet Shehu along with several black and white photos taken in the congress. Besides the latest news from Albania, this issue includes Elena Kadare's short story 'Voice from the Dead', Veniamin Toçi's text on the process of the transformation of urban craft cooperatives into state property in 1968-1969, a long critical review against the "distortions and falsification" of Michael Kaser and Adi Schnytzer's book *Albania — A Uniquely Socialist Economy*.

ALBANIAN LIFE: QUARTERLY JOURNAL OF THE ALBANIAN SOCIETY, NO. 22, THIRD QUARTER 1982

Ilford: The Albanian Society, 1982.
60p. 22 × 14,8 cm.

Obituary of musicologist Albert Lancaster "Bert" Lloyd (1908-1982), who was the President of the Albanian Society. Description by Bill Bland and Steve Day of the visit of the delegation of Albanian Society in Albania in May 1982. Correspondence about Lloyd, describing his work as advocating for contemporary Albania where "culture was not ossified". A poem by Ismail Kadare, and essays on the National Library in Tirana and development of education in Albania. Ten pages of bibliography, in English language, on Albania compiled by John L. Broom.

ALBANIAN LIFE: QUARTERLY JOURNAL OF THE ALBANIAN SOCIETY, NO. 21, SECOND QUARTER 1982

Ilford: The Albanian Society, 1982.
55p. 22 × 14,8 cm.

The issue opens with Fan Noli's analysis of Hamlet, which follows with Ken Smith's essay 'Museums in Albania'. There are a few poems, including Migjeni's anti-religious poem titled 'Scandalous Song' and a long historical survey of the American Technical School in Tirana by William B. Bland. Shkolla Teknike was opened by the American Junior Red Cross in 1921 and it operated until 1933. Bland's short introductory note is intriguing: "When I first visited Albania in 1961 I was struck by the fact that the fluent interpreters allocated to me spoke with a pronounced American accent. They had never been to the United States and had learned the English language from Albanian teachers who had studied in the Technical School, who passed their acquitted accent and spelling to the next generation."

ALBANIAN LIFE: QUARTERLY JOURNAL OF THE ALBANIAN SOCIETY, NO. 23, 1982

Ilford: The Albanian Society, 1982.
48p. 22 × 14,8 cm.

Two texts by Fan Noli, 'That Lout Schubert' (1928) and 'Concerning Don Quixote' (1931). Noli declaratively writes: "Read Don Quixote. You will see him at every step, in every corner." Renee Anderson, 'Five years in Albania', translated from Swedish from *Albanien och Vi* (Albania and Us). In the correspondence section, John L. Broom criticises *Albanian Life* journal as "reporting only the favourable aspects of life under the Hoxha regime and ignoring all that can be said on the debit side." The editorial committee in their lengthy reply address some of the accusations involving issues such as income per capita, real wages, civil and political liberties, holidays abroad, persecution of religion, and torture, concluding that if anything ever is written about Albania are always about its debit side and that anything "can be said" about Albania, which is frequently done.

ALBANIAN LIFE
50p

Quarterly Journal of the Albanian Society
New Series, No. 21 Second Quarter, 1982

ALBANIAN LIFE
50p

Quarterly Journal of the Albanian Society
New Series No. 22 Third Quarter, 1982

SPECIAL CONGRESS ISSUE

ALBANIAN LIFE
50p

Quarterly Journal of the Albanian Society
New Series, No. 20 First Quarter, 1982

ALBANIAN LIFE
50p

Quarterly Journal of the Albanian Society
No. 23   No. 4, 1982

ALBANIAN LIFE

50p

Quarterly Journal of the Albanian Society
No. 24   No.1, 1983

ALBANIAN LIFE

50 p

N°29   N° 2 1984
JOURNAL OF THE ALBANIAN SOCIETY

ALBANIAN LIFE

50p.

Quarterly Journal of the Albanian Society
N° 27   N° 4 1983

ALBANIAN LIFE

50 p

No.30   No3 1984
JOURNAL OF THE ALBANIAN SOCIETY

ALBANIAN LIFE: QUARTERLY JOURNAL OF THE ALBANIAN SOCIETY, NO. 24, 1983

Ilford: The Albanian Society, 1983.
48p. 22 × 14,8 cm.

A lengthy introduction by the new President of Albanian Society, Martin Smith's 'Albania's Struggle for Independence', concluding with "the call upon the British government to return forthwith the Albanian gold held in London since 1945 and so enable relations between Britain and Albania to be normalised". Steve Day's short reportage on the Bushat Cooperative Farm, near Shkodra; Kico Blushi's story 'Woman's Heart'; Xhevahir Spahiu's poem 'The Girl from Kosovo'. The editorial essay 'Approaches to Albania from "East" and "West"', tackles how the US and the USSR are not differing in their slander of Albania.

ALBANIAN LIFE: JOURNAL OF THE ALBANIAN SOCIETY, NO. 29, 1984

Ilford: The Albanian Society, 1984.
49p. 21 × 14,8 cm.

This issue opens with a rather interesting account of Bill Bland's recent visit to Albania. Bland visited many cities and villages during his stay in the country and met with many people including the officials of the cultural institutions. He gives special highlights of his visit to the Greek minority in the South where he learned more about their political and cultural rights; and to his meeting with a judge of the Supreme Court where he learns about the Penal System (he is informed that during the whole 1982, only 111 people in the country were sentenced to some penalty for criminal offences). At one point he compares a ticket price for cinema in Albania (around 15 English pence) to one in London (2.5 pounds). Among others, the issue includes another text of Bland on the trade unions of Albania, a text on the instrument *kalushun,* several short stories and poems, and an account of the Albanian economy between 1983-1984 by Qirjako Mihali.

ALBANIAN LIFE: QUARTERLY JOURNAL OF THE ALBANIAN SOCIETY, NO. 27, 1983

Ilford: The Albanian Society, 1983.
45p. 22 × 14,8 cm.

The opening essay by Norbert Steinmayr 'The Current Situation in Kosovo' is a detailed analysis of the oppression of Albanians in Yugoslavia. It gives examples of the official Yugoslav (predominantly Serbian) press' slander of the Albanians' right to express their own culture, which is the culture of the 80% of the population in Kosovo. The Albanian Society joins the worldwide condemnation of the Yugoslav repression in the tragic events in Kosovo in 1981 and gives its full support to the legitimate demands of the Albanians within Yugoslavia for republican status within the federal Yugoslav state. Dave Smith's reportage essay on the Institute of People's Culture, and Bill Bland's unpublished letters to the *Sunday Times* criticising their coverage of Albania are particularly interesting.

ALBANIAN LIFE: JOURNAL OF THE ALBANIAN SOCIETY, NO. 30, 1984

Ilford: The Albanian Society, 1984.
49p. 21 × 14,8 cm.

After a short editorial on the 40 years anniversary of the liberation, Bill Bland reviews the failed attempt of 1950 "invasion" of Albania by British and American intelligence service. Co-writer of a book on the history of the Anglo-American relations with Albania, Bland reveals this plot based on the recently leaked British secret documents. The issue also includes Bland's long response to a letter directed towards him concerning the social and political roots of atheism in Socialist Albania. Other texts include the history of Albanian language, a short story and a poem, notes on Albanian music and book reviews.

ALBANIAN LIFE: JOURNAL OF THE ALBANIAN SOCIETY, NO. 32, 1985

Ilford: The Albanian Society, 1985.
48p. 21 × 15,5 cm.

The entire issue is dedicated to Enver Hoxha, who died on April 11th, 1985. Including a biographical note, a medical bulletin, the funeral oration by Ramiz Alia, and an interview with Hoxha given to Professor Paul Milliez in December 1984. Steve Day's essay 'British Press-Lies and Speculations' answers to British media which reported Hoxha's death with the title 'Man Who Hated Everybody'.

ALBANIAN LIFE: JOURNAL OF THE ALBANIAN SOCIETY, NO. 35, 1986

Ilford: The Albanian Society, 1986.
48p. 21 × 15,5 cm.

Opening text by Norberto Steinmayr, 'The Corfu Channel Incident', a short intro into the incident on 22 October 1946, when a British warship sailing, without having previously notified, within one mile of Saranda harbour hit mines, which resulted in forty-four deaths. Announced the upcoming book compiled by Bill Bland, 'Miscarriage of Justice', focusing on the incident and the following international court case. Bill Bland's review of Jon Halliday's book *The Artful Albanian: The Memoirs of Enver Hoxha* (1986), applauds the author for taking pains to read carefully a vast amount of historical materials, including Hoxha's writings, but ends with conclusions that are "little different from that of a journalist of *The Sun*."

ALBANIAN LIFE: JOURNAL OF THE ALBANIAN SOCIETY, NO. 34, 1986

Ilford: The Albanian Society, 1986.
48p. 21 × 15,5 cm.

Report on a national meeting of the Albanian Society held in London, November, 1985. The new committee was elected with Dave Smith as a member, who organised a concert of Albanian café music after the meeting. A long text by Norberto Steinmayr 'Enver Hoxha and the Liberation War'.

ALBANIAN LIFE: JOURNAL OF THE ALBANIAN SOCIETY, NO. 36, 1986

Ilford: The Albanian Society, 1986.
48p. 21 × 15,5 cm.

Bill Bland's lengthy and detailed text 'The Theatre in Albania' claims that "the Party of Labour maintains that good art must be realist in form and, in the case of contemporary art, must accord with the principles of socialist humanism." In the Correspondence section John L. Broms criticises Bill Bland's negative review of Jon Halliday's book, calling it naive as they are supportive of the regime, which "continue to deny that Stalin was responsible for some of the most hideous atrocities of our bloodstained century." Bland answers the letter with a long essay including headings on the cult of personality, Lenin's testament, the public trials of the 30s, and the historical debates which he continued to pursue in the nineties.

ALBANIAN LIFE

50 p

MEMORIAL ISSUE

No.32   No.2 1985

JOURNAL OF THE ALBANIAN SOCIETY

ALBANIAN LIFE

50 p

Nº 35   Nº 2 1986

JOURNAL OF THE ALBANIAN SOCIETY

ALBANIAN LIFE

50 p

Nº 34   Nº 1 1986

JOURNAL OF THE ALBANIAN SOCIETY

ALBANIAN LIFE

50 p

No 36 No 3 1986

JOURNAL OF THE ALBANIAN SOCIETY

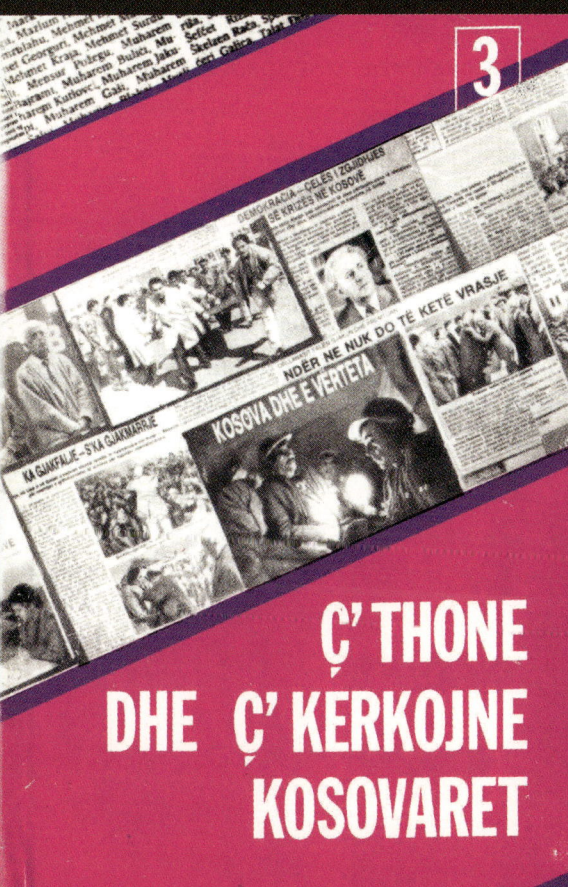

SOCIO-POLITICAL STUDIES, NO. 3, 1986

Tirana, 1986.
251 p. 23 × 15,5 cm.

Theoretical journal published by the Institute of Marxist-Leninist Studies at the Central Committee of the Party of Labour of Albania. In this issue there are three previously unpublished PLA documents; studies and articles by 'senior scientific workers', including, among others, an article by Refik Kucaj, 'The contribution of the Albanian people to the Anti-fascist World War (1939-1945) cannot be obscured by bourgeois-revisionist historiography', and Priamo Bollano's 'Criticism of some bourgeois-revisionist theories on the place and role of the commodity-money relations in socialism'. Includes bibliography of Albanian socio-political publications translated into foreign language during the period 1983-1986.

Ç'THONË DHE Ç'KËRKOJNË KOSOVARËT VOL 2

Tirana: 8 Nëntori, 1990.
389p. 21 × 14 cm.

The second volume of *What the Kosovars Say and Demand* is published just a few months after the first book and it reflects the political repression, police violence, and Albanophobia which intensified between those months. The articles, interviews, open letters, and comments which are brought together in this book were written by Kosovo Albanian intellectuals and published in the various Yugoslavian press, including *Rilindja, Danas, Zëri i Amerikës, Alternativa,* etc.

Ç'THONË DHE Ç'KËRKOJNË KOSOVARËT

Tirana: 8 Nëntori, 1989.
373p. 21 × 14 cm.

What the Kosovars Say and Demand is published at a time when Serbian chauvinism took an aggressive turn in Yugoslavia. This volume brings together studies, articles, interviews, and comments on the reasons and effects of the political violence against Kosovo Albanians, published in various Yugoslavian press at the end of the 1980s. All texts were written by Kosovo Albanian intellectuals.

Ç'THONË DHE Ç'KËRKOJNË KOSOVARËT VOL 3

Tirana: 8 Nëntori, 1990.
491p. 20 × 13,5 cm.

This is the final Albanian language volume of *What the Kosovars Say and Demand* published a few months after the second one, in July. It includes the Declaration of the Constitutional Assembly of Kosovo, which was declared on the 2nd of July and published in Rilindja Newspaper the next day, as well as many other articles, interviews, and comments by intellectual figures such as Fehmi Agani, Adem Demaçi, Rexhep Qosja, Ibrahim Rugova, etc.

PHOTOGRAPHY UNMASKS
Fotografia demaskon

On the verge of the neoliberal restructuring of the capitalist system, Enver Hoxha declared that "the capitalist world has plunged into a great crisis." In his speech delivered at the meeting of the General Council in 1978, published the same year in *Proletarian Democracy is Genuine Democracy*, he claimed that the theses of Marx and Lenin on capitalism and imperialism, let aside from being outdated, were accurate more than ever before. Capitalism and imperialism were in "a process of deterioration." To emerge from the crisis, "these champions of the old order loudly advertise the 'fight against terrorism', for the prevention of the revolts and the revolution of the masses of the working people against the capitalist order, or the fight against 'riots,' as they call them." The capitalist and "revisionist countries [...] are seething with mass protests," which are masked by media and police violence.

Later, in his political diary, *The Superpowers*, Hoxha wrote that "the awakening of the peoples of the world is an incontestable fact" — at the beginning of the eighties, he predicted that the coming decade would be that of uprisings that would continue to give "bad fevers" to the imperialists of the developed Western countries.

The images presented in these pages are taken from the biweekly *Zëri i Rinisë* (The Voice of Youth) published in 1984 and 1985 by the Central Committee of the Union of the Working Youth of Albania. The photographs aimed to show the ongoing riots, protests, and strikes from all around the capitalist world and 'unmask' the state violence, inherent in the capitalist system, against the masses.

Me anë të kësaj pamjeje krijon idenë se në ç'gjendje është jetesa e masave në Filipine. Prandaj masat e gjera popullore, rinia studentore (foto 2) janë hedhur në demonstrata të fuqishme kundër regjimit fashist të Markosit.

Through this image, one understands an impression of the living conditions for the masses in the Philippines at the time. It was against such conditions that students, youth (image 2), and the broader population entered into powerful demonstrations against Ferdinand Marcos' fascist regime.

Pjesëmarrja e grave punonjëse portugeze në luftën klasore kundër kapitalit po rritet e forcohet. Në foto: pamje e një demonstrate të grave.

The participation of Portuguese women in the class struggle against the capitalist system was growing and strengthening. This image depicts one such demonstration by women.

Demonstratë e punonjësve spanjollë kundër imperializmit amerikan dhe pranisë së tij ushtarake në territorin e këtij vendi.

Demonstration of Spanish workers against American imperialism, and its military presence in the country.

The youth responds with determined protests against the violence and denial of democratic rights.

In many cities of Britain, people organise solidarity demonstrations, supporting the miners' strike, whose jobs are short to be endangered by the closing of the mines. Margaret Thatcher's government uses brutal police violence against the working demonstrators, here depicted in Nottinghamshire, one of the most important regions for coal extraction.

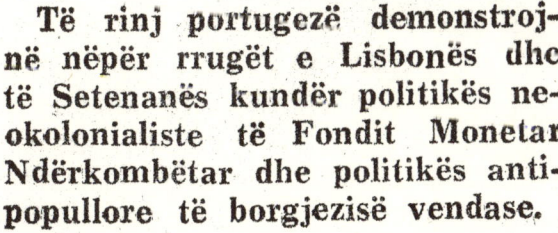

Të rinj portugezë demonstrojnë nëpër rrugët e Lisbonës dhe të Setenanës kundër politikës neokolonialiste të Fondit Monetar Ndërkombëtar dhe politikës antipopullore të borgjezisë vendase.

Young Portuguese people protest in the streets of Lisbon and Setenave shipyard, in Setúbal, against the neo-colonial politics of the International Monetary Fund (IMF) and the anti-popular politics of the bourgeoisie.

RFGJ: Të rinjtë demonstrojnë me parullat: «Jashtë nga blloku i NATO-s» dhe «Punë e arsimim në vend të «Pershingëve»».

In West Germany, young people demonstrate with banners reading "Out of the NATO block" and "Work and Education instead of 'Pershing'."

Në shumë vende të Amerikës Latine, ku sundojnë klikat fashiste, masat jetojnë në një gjendje të mjerë.

In many parts of Latin America where fascist cliques rule, people live in miserable conditions.

18.000 gra e të reja gjermanoperëndimore protestojnë kundër papunësisë.

18,000 women in West Germany protest against unemployment.

Gratë në botën e kapitalit janë hedhur në barrikadat e luftës klasore. Ato kanë marshuar kohët e fundit në rrugët e kryeqyteteve të ndryshme duke kërkuar të drejtat e tyre, duke protestuar kundër diskriminimit që u bëhet atyre në të gjitha fushat.

In the capitalist West, women have committed themselves to the barricades of class war, marching in the streets of capital cities, demanding their rights and protesting against the discrimination they face in all areas of life.

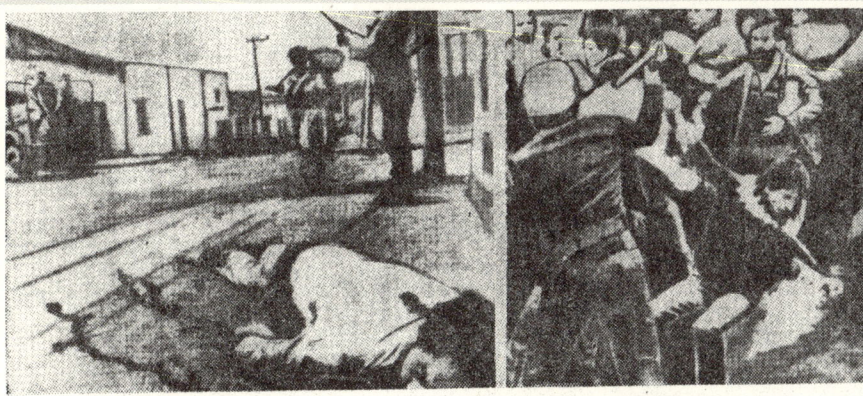

Sot, në shumë vende të botës, regjimet antipopullore ushtrojnë dhunë fashiste ndaj masave të gjera të popullit. Ja se çfarë tregon fotografia e parë; «Skuadronet e vdekjes» në Salvador lënë çdo ditë viktima të reja nëpër rrugët e qyteteve. Por, valës së ringjalljes së fashizmit, popujt dhe rinia i përgjigjen me demonstrata e përleshje të përgjakshme. Një pamje të tillë paraqet fotografia e dytë.

In many countries, anti-popular regimes use fascist violence against the people. This first image illustrates that every day "Death Squads" leave behind new victims in the streets of the city of San Salvador. To this wave of the resurrection of fascism, the people and youth responded with demonstrations and bloody fights, as the second image shows.

Me politikën e tyre luftënxitëse, të dy superfuqitë, SHBA dhe BS, kanë intensifikuar garën e shfrenuar të armatimit bërthamor e konvencional. Këtë veprimtari të ethshme luftënxitëse po përpiqen ta mbulojnë me manevra propagandistike, fjalime dhe mbledhje diplomatike, pa bukë për gjoja çarmatim. Por popuj e Evropës e të botës, të ndërgjegjshëm për pasojat e rënda që mbart politika luftënxitëse e këtyre dy superfuqive, po e kundërshtojnë atë me vendosmëri përmes protestash e demonstratash masive. Në foton që po botojmë masat dhe rinia amerikane protestojnë me parullat «Fonde për vende pune, jo për luftën».

With their politics of war instigation, both superpowers the USA and the USSR have intensified their rampant race for nuclear armament and the bolstering of conventional military. They're trying to cover up this war instigation with propagandistic manoeuvres, speeches, and diplomatic meetings, for alleged disarmament. But the countries and people of Europe, aware of the consequences of the war instigation politics, are opposing these two superpowers with strong protests and massive demonstrations. In this image, the masses and American youth are protesting under the banners "Funds for jobs, not for war".

45 000 demonstrues të qytetit të Mensfildit mbështesin grevën e minatorëve britanikë.

45,000 demonstrate in support of the British miners' strike in the city of Mansfield.

Të gjithë popujt e botës janë ngritur në këmbë dhe kundërshtojnë me forcë përgatitjet e ethshme për luftë dhe politikën luftënxitëse të dy superfuqive - SHBA dhe BS, si dhe të shteteve të tjera imperialiste.

All the people of the world have risen and are strongly opposing the feverish preparations for war as well as the war instigation politics of the two superpowers, the USA and USSR, and other imperialist countries.

Pjesëmarrje e grave kiliane në luftën klasore kundër diktaturës gjakatare të Pinoçetit.

The participation of Chilean women in the class war against the bloody dictatorship of Augusto Pinochet.

Punonjës e të rinj japonezë demonstrojnë kundër politikës agresive të imperializmit amerikan, kundër bashkëpunimit përherë e më të ngushtë japono-amerikan në fushën ushtarake.

Workers and Japanese youngsters demonstrate against the aggressive politics of American imperialism as well as against the close Japan-American cooperation in the military field.

Lufta e proletariatit dhe rinisë portugeze kundër shtypjes dhe shfrytëzimit kapitalist po merr përmasa përherë e më të mëdha. Në foto: Pamje nga një demonstratë e zhvilluar kohët e fundit në Lisbonë.

The war of the proletariat and Portuguese youth against oppression and capitalist exploitation is getting bigger every time. The image: A recent demonstration in Lisbona.

Demonstrata të të rinjve britanikë në mbështetje të grevës së minatorëve.

A demonstration of British youth in support of the miners' strike.

Demonstrata masive të masave në Britani, RFGJ dhe Portugali.

Massive popular demonstrations in Britain and the Federal Republic of Germany.

Të rinj britanikë protestojnë kundër politikës antipopullore të Theçerit.

British youth protest against the anti-popular politics of Thatcher.

Demonstratë e fuqishme e të rinjve spanjollë, zhvilluar në Madrid kohët e fundit.

A recent powerful demonstration of Spanish youth in Madrid.

Kërkesat e vazhdueshme të rinisë në vendet kapitaliste: punë, arsimim e të drejta demokratike.

The persistent demands of the youth in capitalist countries: jobs, education and democratic rights.

FOTOGRAFIA DEMASKON. Një polic qëllon për vdekje një të ri veriirlandez në protestat e ditëve të fundit.

THE PHOTOGRAPHY UNMASKS: A member of the police shoots dead a Northern Irish boy in the last-year protest.

Rritja e taksave në SHBA ka ngjallur një lëvizje të gjerë proteste. Në foto: një nga demonstratat e zhvilluara nëpër rrugët e Çikagos për të kundërshtuar rritjen e mëtejshme të kostos së jetesës.

The tax increase in the USA spurs a wide protest movement. In the image: one of the demonstrations in the streets of Chicago, to oppose the further increase to the cost of living.

Politika reaksionare dhe antipopullore e Indira Gandit ka ngjallur zemërimin e masave të rinisë, të cilat po hidhen në greva e demonstrata të fuqishme proteste. Për shtypjen e tyre qeveria ka mobilizuar forca të shumta policore. Në foto: Forcat e policisë duke sulmuar me shkopinj masat e demonstruesve.

The reactionary and anti-popular politics of Indira Gandhi has revived the anger of the youth masses, who are throwing strikes and powerful demonstrations. To oppress them, the government has mobilized several police forces. In the image: Police forces attacking the masses of demonstrators with sticks.

1984

The bourgeoisie uses ferocious violence toward the masses and young people who demand their rights and democratic freedom.

West Germany: The masses protest: "Jobs for everybody. Foreign troops to be withdrawn from the country."

Many young people participating in the long British miners' strike, keep on their shoulders the suffering and social injustice of the Thatcher government.

In the streets of Montréal, many young people demonstrate for their right to work and other social rights.

Lufta klasore e proletariatit portugez kundër krizës që rëndon mbi kurrizin e tij po merr përmasa gjithnjë e më të mëdha. Në foto: Pamje e një demonstrate të zhvilluar kohët e fundit.

The class and proletariat struggle of Portuguese people is growing ever more. In this image: A recent demonstration.

RFGJ: Marshim proteste kundër dislokimit të armëve bërthamore në Evropë.

SHBA: Dhunë policore kundër popullsisë zezake.

West Germany: Marching against the dislocation of nuclear weapons in Europe.

USA: Police violence against black people

Më shumë se 20 000 studentë britanikë zhvilluan kohët e fundit një demonstratë proteste nëpër rrugët e Londrës kundër rënies së vazhduoshme të nivelit të jetesës.

Në Salvador, si në shumë vende të tjera ku sundojnë klikat reaksionare, mungojnë edhe kushtet më elementare për jetesë. Grup fëmijësh duke pritur radhën për të mbushur ujë.

In El Salvador, just as in many other places where reactionary cliques are leading, there is a lack of basic conditions for life. A group of children waiting for water.

More than 20, 000 British students organise a demonstration in the streets of London, against the continuous decline in living standards.

Forca të policisë kolumbiane arrestojnë me dhunë një të ri demonstrues në rrugët e Bogotës.

Colombian police forces violently arrest a young demonstrator in the streets of Bogotá.

1984

Regjimi fashist i Pinoçetit mundohet t'i mbysë me dhunë të egër policore demonstratat e fuqishme popullore në rrugët e Santiagos.

In the streets of Santiago, the fascist regime of Pinochet tries to stop the powerful demonstrations with brutal police violence.

Përveç grevave e demonstratave, minatorët britanikë kanë organizuar edhe shumë mitingje proteste. Në foto: Minatorët e minierës Tillmënstoun të Kentit duke zhvilluar një miting proteste.

Besides the strikes and demonstrations, British miners have organised many protest meetings. In the image: The Miners of Tilmanstone organising a protest meeting.

Forca të policisë britanike duke arrestuar një minator grevist.

British police forces arrest a strike miner.

Në qytetet e ndryshme të Kilit dhuna e ushtruar nga forcat e policisë sa vjen e bëhet më e ashpër. Viktima të kësaj dhune janë shpesh të rinjtë kilianë që kundërshtojnë me forcë politikën e shtypjes e të terrorit të ushtruar nga diktatori Pinoçet. NË FOTO: Forca të policisë kiliane duke qëlluar mbi një grup demonstruesish.

In several cities in Chile, violence perpetrated by police forces becomes more and more severe. Often, the victims of this violence are young Chileans who oppose the political force and terror exerted by Pinochet. In the image: Chilean police forces shooting a group of demonstrators.

Trupat policore spanjolle ushtrojnë dhunë e terror kundër një demonstrate të punonjësve në Hueska.

Spanish police troops exert violence and terror in a demonstration of workers in Huesca.

Në foto: Punëtorët e kantierit detar të Hamburgut në RFGJ duke protestuar kundër pushimeve masive nga puna dhe shtimit të papunësisë në vend.

Image: Shipyard workers of Hamburg in West Germany protest against the massive job losses and increasing unemployment in the country.

Demonstratë proteste e punonjësve britanikë.

Demonstrations and protests of British workers.

Lufta e popullit afgan intensifikohet çdo ditë e më shumë. Në foto: patriotët afganë nisen për luftim.

The war of Afghan people increases every day and more. In the image: Afghans embark on combat.

Punonjës dhe të rinj portugezë demonstrojnë kundër FMN-së

Portuguese workers and young people demonstrate against the IMF (International Monetary Fund).

Gjatë gjithë grevës së minatorëve britanikë është ndjerë si kurrë më parë fryma e lartë e solidaritetit punëtor për të mbrojtur minatorët nga sulmet e policisë.

Like never before throughout the British miners' strike, there was a strong feeling of workers' solidarity to protect them from any police attack.

Në fotot: Gjendje e rëndë e jetesës së popullsisë kolumbiane. Të rinj kolumbianë demonstrojnë kundër shfrytëzimit kapitalist.

In the image: The hard conditions of living of the Colombian population. Young Colombians demonstrate against capitalist exploitation.

Të rinjtë në qytetin Tuikinhem të Britanisë protestojnë kundër turneut të shoqatës angleze të futbollit dhe regbisë në Afrikën e Jugut.

Young people in Twickenham, North London, protest against the English Football and Rugby Association's tournaments in South Africa.

Humbje të konsiderueshme u janë shkaktuar pushtuesve sovjetikë në Afganistan nga lufta e paepur e luftëtarëve afganë. Në foto: Një luftëtar afgan në pozicion luftimi në një terren shkëmbor.

Punonjësit portugezë zhvillojnë një demonstratë të fuqishme kundër shtypjes dhe shfrytëzimit kapitalist në rrugët e Lisbonës.

Significant losses were inflicted on the Soviet invaders in Afghanistan by the relentless warfare of Afghan fighters. An Afghan fighter in combat position on rocky terrain.

On the streets of Lisbon, Portuguese workers direct a strong demonstration against oppression and capitalist exploitation.

Demonstratë masive në Hamburg të RFGJ-së. Të rinjtë gjermanoperëndimorë, të vënë përkrah masave të tjera të punëtorëve, protestojnë e solidarizohen me luftën e punonjësve të kantjerit të anijeve.

A massive demonstration in Hamburg. Young West Germans put together with other masses of workers protest, and show solidarity with the struggle of the shipyard workers.

Gra dhe të reja portugeze protestojnë kundër shtypjes dhe shfrytëzimit

Young Portuguese girls and women protest against oppression and exploitation.

1984

Demonstratë e fuqishme proteste e të rinjve brazilianë në San Paolo kundër politikës antipopullore të regjimit në fuqi në këtë vend.

A demonstration of young Brazilians in São Paolo against the anti-popular politics of the regime of the Military Dictatorship.

Gjatë turbullirave në Majami të SHBA-së policia arrestoi një numër të rinjsh që protestonin kundër brutalitetit të policisë ndaj popullsisë së pafajshme zezake. Në foto një i ri zezak duke u kapur me forcë nga policia.

During riots in Miami, USA, the police arrested a number of young people protesting against police brutality toward the innocent black population. In the image: a young black man being forcibly caught by the police.

Rritet përditë lufta e rinisë në vendet kapitaliste.

The young people's war against capitalism grows every day.

Demonstrata proteste kundër shtypjes dhe shfrytëzimit kapitalist të të rinjve gjermanoperëndimorë dhe portugezë.

Demonstrations and protests against the oppression and exploitation of West German and Portuguese youth.

- Masat e gjera punonjëse kanadeze kundërshtojnë me forcë shndërrimin e territorit të Kanadasë në një poligon provash për raketat amerikane «Kruiz» Në foto: Demonstratë e madhe proteste në Vankuver, në të cilën morën pjesë mbi 100 mijë vetë.

Large masses of Canadian workers strongly oppose the transformation of Canadian territory into a test site for US "Cruise" missiles. In the photo: A large protest demonstration in Vancouver attended by over 100,000 people.

1984

Demonstratë proteste e të rinjve anglezë kundër shtypjes dhe shfrytëzimit kapitalist.

Demonstrations and protests of English youth against capitalist oppression and exploitation.

Të rinjtë në vendet borgjeze protestojnë kundër shkurtimit të fondeve sociale dhe pakësimit të vendeve të punës.

Young people in bourgeois countries are protesting against cuts in social funding and jobs.

Foto 1: Të rinj gjermanoperëndimorë në demonstratë. Foto 2: Trupa të policisë portugeze në Lisbonë, të gatshëm për të mbytur me dhunë revoltat e punonjësve.

Image 1: West German youth protest.
Image 2: Portuguese police troops in Lisbon, ready to violently quell workers' revolts.

Masa të rinisë portugeze protestojnë së bashku me punonjësit.

Portuguese youth protest together with workers.

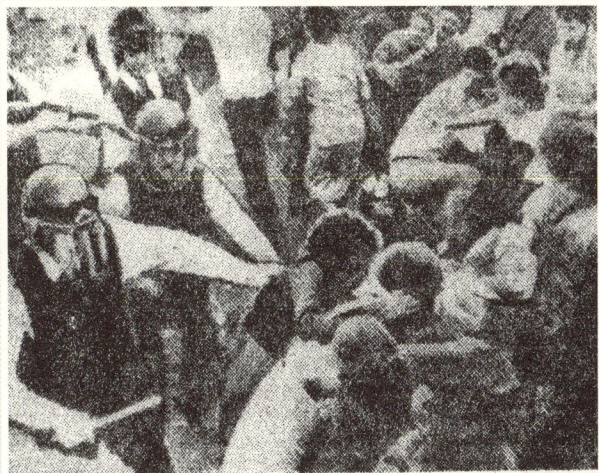

«Amerikanë shkoni në shtëpinë tuaj». Të rinj gjermanoperëndimorë protestojnë kundër pranisë amerikane në vendin e tyre.

Rrugët e Belfastit shpesh bëhen arena të përleshjeve të ashpra të policisë me demonstruesit, të cilët kundërshtojnë me vendosmëri politikën e shtypjes e të terrorit në vend.

"Americans, go home." Young West Germans protest against the American presence in their country.

The streets of Belfast become arenas of fierce police clashes with demonstrators, who strongly oppose British policy, repression and terror.

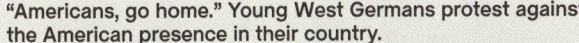

Të rinjtë londinezë protestojnë kundër turpit të botës – racizmit. Të rinj japonezë dënojnë përgatitjet për luftë të dy superfuqive – SHBA dhe BS, si dhe të vendeve të tjera imperialiste.

Young Londoners protest against the shame of the world — racism. Japanese youth condemn war preparations of two superpowers — the USA and the USSR, as well as other countries.

Lëvizja antibërthamore në RFGJ ka marrë përpjesëtime të mëdha. Pamja nga një prej demonstratave kundër dislokimit të raketave bërthamore në tokën gjermane.

Në Nju London (Britani) u dërguan forca të shumta të policisë për të shpërndarë demonstruesit, të cilët protestonin kundër ardhjes në vend të nëndetëseve të reja atomike amerikane të tipit «Xhorxhia», të afta për të mbajtur në bord raketa bërthamore. Në foto: forca të policisë duke arrestuar pjesëmarrës të kësaj demonstrate.

The anti-nuclear movement in West Germany takes on larger proportions. View from one of the demonstrations against the deployment of nuclear missiles on German land.

Protesta të ditëve të fundit të të rinjve portugezë.

In New London (Britain), numerous police forces were sent to disperse demonstrators, who protest against the arrival of the new American atomic submarines "George", capable of keeping nuclear missiles on board. In the photo: police forces arresting the participants of this demonstration.

Të rinjtë skocezë demonstrojnë në rrugët e Glaskout në mbështetje të luftës së minatorëve angleze, e cila po merr përpjesëtime gjithnjë e më të mëdha.

Scottish youth demonstrate in the streets of Glasgow in support of the English miners' strike, now at its peak.

Trupa të policisë kiliane duke arrestuar pjesëmarës të demonstratave në Santiago.

Chilean police troops arrest protesters in Santiago.

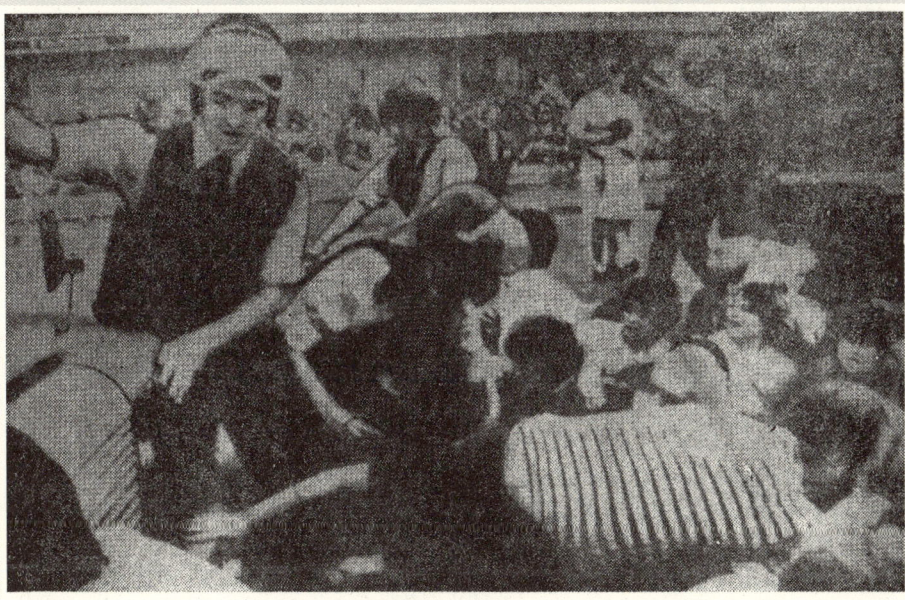

Forcat pushtuese britanike në Irlandën ë Veriut vazhdojnë me egërsi të pashembullt represionet e dhunën kundër atdhetarëve irlandezë që kundërshtojnë shtypjen e terrorin në vend. Në foto: trupat e pushtuesve britanikë duke shpërndarë me forcë një grup demonstruesish në Belfast.

With unprecedented ferocity, the British occupation forces in Northern Ireland continue their repression and violence against the Irish patriots who oppose the suppression by terror in the country. In the image: troops of the British occupiers dispersing a group of demonstrators in Belfast.

Përleshje e ashpër e minatorëve grevistë anglezë me policinë. A fierce fight between English miners and the police.

Vuajtje e mjerim – ja se ç'u siguron sistemi kapitalist miliona fëmijëve në botë. Suffering and misery — what the capitalist system provides to millions of children around the world.

Të rinjtë kilianë përleshen me forcat e policisë. Young Chileans clash with armed police.

40 mijë të rinj dhe punëtorë demonstrojnë në rrugët e Londrës.

40,000 young people and workers demonstrate in the streets of London.

Të rinjtë evropianoperëndimorë kundërshtojnë politikën luftënxitëse të dy superfuqive.

Western European youth oppose the warmongering policies of the two superpowers, the USA and the USSR.

Demonstratë e të rinjve spanjollë kundër NATO-s.

A demonstration of the Spanish youth against NATO.

1985

Palestinian youth protest against Zionist terror in the occupied territories.

Progressive youth raise their voices in protest against ongoing and escalating preparations for war by the two superpowers.

Afghan patriots, involved in the People's Liberation Army, put up a strong resistance to the imperialist Soviet Army.

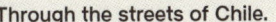

Through the streets of Chile.

Protests in the streets of New York against the Reagan government's measures to cut social funds.

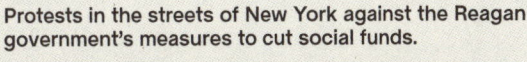

Demonstrations by young Irish people condemning the continuation of predatory neocolonialist policies from the Thatcher government. Such demonstrations also take place in London.

Nga një demonstratë e të rinjve azanianë afër Durbanit kundër politikës së egër të aparteidit të regjimit të Bothas.

From a demonstration of Azania youth near Durban against the brutal political apartheid of the Botha regime.

Pamje nga një demonstratë e të rinjve studentë britanikë para burgut të Pentovilit për të kundërshtuar burgosjen e shokëve të tyre të universitetit politeknik të Londrës.

A view from a demonstration of young British students in front of the HMP Prison Pentonville to oppose the imprisonment of their friends from the London Polytechnic University.

Demonstratë proteste e të rinjve për të drejta e liri demokratike.

A youth demonstration for democratic rights and freedom.

Të rinj spanjollë protestoinë për të dreitat e tvre.

Young Spanish people protest for their rights.

Të rinj portugezë duke protestuar kundër papunësisë dhe për të drejta të tjera sociale.

Young Portuguese people protest against unemployment and for other social rights.

Të rinj demonstrues afrikanojugorë protestojnë kundër politikës së Reganit në përkrahje të regjimit të urryer të aparteidit në vendin e tyre.

Young South African demonstrators protest against Reagan's policies in support of the apartheid regime in their country.

A group of young Spaniards burning the American flag in protest against the aggressive policies of the Reagan administration.

A demonstration of English youth at the Greenham Common RAF military base. Police arrested 40 of them. There are 4.5 million unemployed young people in the European Common Market. In the photo: Demonstration of West German youth against mass layoffs.

Protest against the policy of "tightening the belt", that is, throwing the burden of the crisis on the working class.

A protest march in front of the US Embassy in Managua, Nicaragua, organised by young people.

A view of a demonstration in the streets of London, where one of the slogans reads: "No police state!"

Azanian students protesting against apartheid.

Demonstrations in Chicago against American support for the apartheid regime in South Africa.

Të rinjtë britanikë protestojnë kundër politikës raciste të qeverisë së Theçerit. Në foto: Pamje nga një demonstratë e organizuar kohët e fundit në Old Bejlej të Britanisë.

Young British people protest against the racist policies of the Thatcher government. In the image: View from a demonstration organised outside the Old Bailey Criminal Court in London.

Fotografia dëshmon: Jetë e mjerë për banorët me ngjyrë në Afrikën e Jugut.

The photography proves it: People of colour in South Africa live in oppressive conditions.

Demonstratë e të rinjve kanadezë për të drejtat arsimore.

A demonstration of Black Canadians for educational rights.

South African youth protest against apartheid.

Terror racist kundër popullit dhe rinisë namibiane

"RACIST TERROR AGAINST THE NAMIBIAN PEOPLE AND YOUTH"

Young Filipinos express their strong opposition to the antipopular and pro-American policies of the Marcos regime.

1985

Rinia në vendet kapitaliste demonstron për liri e të drejta sociale, si dhe kundër përgatitjeve për uftë.

The youth in capitalist countries demonstrate for freedom and social rights, as well as against escalations towards war.

Miting masiv proteste kundër shtimit të papunësisë në Britani.

A massive meeting and a protest against the rising unemployment in Britain.